Mind-Morph

CHANGE YOUR LIFE
BY CHANGING YOUR MIND

CHRIS DOYLE

Copyright © 2020 Chris Doyle

All rights reserved. This book or parts thereof may not be reproduced in any form, stored in any retrieval system, or transmitted in any form by any means—electronic, mechanical, photocopy, recording, or otherwise—without prior written permission of the publisher, except as provided by United States of America copyright law. For permission requests, write to the publisher, at "Attention: Permissions Coordinator," at the address below.

ISBN: 978-0-578-22852-5 (eBook)
ISBN: 978-0-578-22851-8 (Paperback)

Cover Design by Meena Dhyani, www.creativewebbers.com.
Cover Image by Evgeny Terentev, www.istockphoto.com/portfolio/blackjack3d.

Printed by Kindle Direct Publishing, Inc, in the United States of America

First print edition 2020.

Chris Doyle, Mind-Morph
P.O. Box 432
Medina, TN 38355

www.mind-morph.com
info@mind-morph.com

For many, a belief in what is possible is the difference between success and failure. What if there is a change of mind – of belief, to one which says that **everything is possible**?

How would *your* life change if the only thing in front of you is the possibility?

What would the world become if a billion people experience a change of mind?

Embrace the vision.

Dedication

To Ryan, Danelle, Christopher, and Jayden, who are some of the keys on my universal keychain, and who I believe have the heart, might, mind, and spirit to fill their lives with abundance.

Appreciation

Family and friends who listened, supported, read, commented, critiqued, and who continue to deliver the Mind-Morph message, I am sincerely indebted for your patience, and the generosity of your time.

Acknowledgements

Those who helped make this book a reality! My deepest gratitude and a heartfelt thank YOU!

Carrie Clarke, J.D., Coach
www.nextlevelcoachconsult.com

Candace Schilling, Editor
www.candaceschilling.com

Meena Dhyani, Graphic and Web Designer
www.creativewebbers.com

Jay Nocera, Cartoonist
www.nichecartoons.com

CONTENTS

Introduction: Mind-Morph 101
- The Mind-Morph Way 2
- Your Morph-Star 3
- The Mind-Morph Mechanism 3
- The ABCs of the Mind-Morph Mechanism 8

Chapter 1: 7 *Pretty Simple* Fundamentals to Change Your Life
- Fundamental #1 – Can You Believe It? 12
- Fundamental #2 – Buckets of Laws 15
- Fundamental #3 – #FlipTheSwitch 20
- Fundamental #4 – Ready, Set, GET 23
- Fundamental #5 – "Action" Isn't a Noun 26
- Fundamental #6 – Reflect, Reset, Realign 29
- Fundamental #7 – A Key to the Universe 33
- What's Your Starting Point? 38

Chapter 2: Can You Believe It?
- Beliefs 41
  - Limiting vs. Non-Limiting Beliefs 42
- Conditioning 43
- Misbeliefs 45
- The Science 47
  - The Placebo Effect 48
  - How the Brain Works 48
- Managing Beliefs 51
  - How to Change Beliefs 52

Chapter 3: Buckets of Laws

Laws of Physics 64
Laws of Society 65
Laws of the Universe 67
Laws of the Spirit 70
How and whom do you ask? 72
YOU have the power to CREATE! 73
Why is it hard to believe? 73
The Science 75
Connectedness 78
Purpose and Perfection 81

Chapter 4: #FlipTheSwitch

The Science 94
    What is Conditioning? 95
    How Were You Conditioned? 97
    Conditioning can be Changed! 97
    How to Change Your Conditioning 99
The Real "Why" 101

Chapter 5: Ready, Set, GET

What is Asking? 112
Adopting a Growth Mindset 114
Following the Resolution Path 116
    What is Your Why? 116
    Reset, Reflect, Realign 117
    Clear the Fear 118
Achievement Annihilators 120
The Science 120

Are You Ready to Receive? 122
A Formula for *Ask* Success 123

Chapter 6: "Action" isn't a Noun
Working Backward 137
Brainstorming 139
Affirmations 141
The Science 145
Time to Get Started 146
Tips to Speed up Results..147

Chapter 7: Reset, Reflect, Realign
Reset..156
    Resetting Techniques 157
Reflect..163
    Reflecting Techniques...164
Realign...167
    Realigning Techniques..168
R-R-R Remedies 172
The Science 177
"Recalibrate" – The Final R..179

Chapter 8: A Key to the Universe
Living Intentionally 190
The Science 191
A New Universal Perspective 195
Mind-Morphed...198

Conclusion: It's a Wrap
    What to Do Next 209

Supplements
    Achievement Annihilators 212
    Take action Survey 215
    Finding My Why 225

The Mind-Morph Water Butterfly 235

Notes & References 237

Introduction

I'm just a regular guy. A normal Joe. No one is more generic than I am. So when someone asks, "How did you make all this happen?" – how I moved from poverty, bankruptcy, and divorce into abundance – it's time to tell my story. As I do, I emphasize for those listening that what I have done, they can also do. Where I have traveled in my life is a journey everyone can make. This path can be taken by anyone of any age, social status, level of poverty or wealth, in any station of life, anywhere in the world.

I am not a psychologist or therapist. I am certainly not a pastor. I am passionate about my beliefs and experiences. I am a living example of someone who has changed his life by changing his mind – changing the way he thinks. I hope you'll find value in these simple fundamentals, see that if I can do it, you can also, and join me on this journey of life transformation and fulfillment.

Mind-Morph 101

About 10 years ago, I found myself in a familiar and difficult place in my life. I was several years into a second marriage, which would not end well, between jobs, dealing with a bunch of debt, and what seemed like no light at the end of the tunnel. You may remember an episode of *Seinfeld* in which George Costanza had an epiphany that everything in his life was the exact opposite of how it should be. All of the things he was doing from day-to-day always produced the same terrible results, so he decided to do the exact opposite of what he would normally do. He changed his regular lunch meal, he talked with a pretty female stranger, and he stood up to bullies – all things he would never have done before. To his delight . . . it worked!

This describes where I was. I felt as if everything I was doing was creating the opposite of whatever I hoped or planned. I remember saying to myself, "I have *got* to change how my mind works! If what I think is going to work isn't working, then I have to change what I *think*." And that's how Mind-Morph began because that's what Mind-Morph is – a *change* of **mind**.

The Mind-Morph Way

Throughout the book, I refer to the "Mind-Morph Way." The Mind-Morph Way refers to the overall philosophy of Mind-Morph. The philosophy of mind-change as I present it. In the next few paragraphs, I describe a particular process (a mechanism) for living the Mind-Morph Way. You can change your life as I have by living according to this particular philosophy.

For example, you'll soon learn the importance of *beliefs* and **believing** as part of the Mind-Morph philosophy. After reading this book, you may have a conversation with a friend and describe an ambitious goal you have set for yourself. Your friend might respond by saying something like, "Do you think you can do it?"

You will answer, "I sincerely believe I can. It's the Mind-Morph Way." If she asks what you mean, you can explain, "I mean that believing it will happen or believing in the possibility of things is part of the philosophy of Mind-Morph. It is the Mind-Morph Way."

Your Morph-Star

As you begin to understand and practice Mind-Morph, I ask you to consider something in your life you would like to achieve. I refer to this as your Morph-Star. Like the North Star, it will serve as a bright, fixed guide during your mind-change journey. Your Morph-Star is one of your deepest desires. It can be an ideal life achievement such as weight loss, finding a job, or developing a lifetime relationship with a spouse. It can be anything that might contribute toward life fulfillment or abundance, such as increased wealth, retirement or business entrepreneurship. Your Morph-Star can be anything you would like to accomplish or change in your life. And, you will soon see that as you get better at living the Mind-Morph Way, you can Mind-Morph anything at any time.

The Mind-Morph Mechanism

"Engage the mechanism." In the movie *For Love of the Game*, professional baseball pitcher Billy Chapel (played by Kevin Costner), would say these words to himself while he was on the pitching mound to get into his *zone*. His zone is that place where he becomes super-focused on his next pitch. While in his zone, he blocks out everything (all of the noise of the crowd, his peripheral view of the fans and other players, the score of the game, the weather), and focuses strictly on the aspects of the next pitch. All he sees are the catcher's mitt, home plate, and the path the baseball would travel once he throws the ball. He concentrates on nothing except the next pitch. Becoming single-minded is his mechanism. That is to say, the process he follows to accomplish a specific task and achieve a specific result. **Engage the mechanism**.

Similarly, there is a "mechanism" for achieving anything you want in life by living the Mind-Morph Way. It is a system – a process – which you can use over and over again. You can use it for achievements of all magnitudes, such as choosing the quickest driving route when you're late to work while attracting all green lights so you make it on time, landing that big promotion even though it may be a little out of your reach, or meeting your soulmate for a lifetime of companionship and happiness.

The mechanism follows the 7 *Pretty Simple* Fundamentals to Change Your Life, which you'll read about in Chapter 1, and here it is:

Conceive   When you've had a brilliant idea, you're facing a challenge, or you have a goal you would like to reach, conceiving is whatever comes to your mind that you would like to achieve. I include **conceiving** and believing together because, in your mind, they usually occur in extremely close succession with one another. For example, you conceive a big, brilliant idea or desire and immediately, you *believe* it is either possible or not possible.

Believe **Believing** means you believe you can achieve, overcome, or accomplish your idea, challenge or goal – your Morph-Star. Living the Mind-Morph Way, you begin to believe in all possibilities for yourself. Soon, there will be nothing you think you can't personally accomplish. Whether the thing you have conceived is meant to be, or not to be for you, you will believe in the *possibility* it can occur. When living the Mind-Morph Way, you will find complete peace, even when those great things you conceive work out differently than you expect.

Decide Once you've envisioned, and you believe in the possibility, you still need to **decide** to take action needed to reach your achievement. Deciding is an important step. Much of what keeps us from succeeding in our efforts is that we may not have fully adopted or embraced the *decision in our minds* that we are going to do it wholeheartedly.

Ask   Once you've decided (or while deciding), you will need to start to **ask**. Begin asking yourself *why* you want what you are seeking, asking God or your Higher Power for help in your success, asking other people for direction, ideas, feedback, and even asking yourself from time-to-time if you're ready to keep at it until you've obtained it.

Act   Finally, you have to **act**. You will find yourself consumed with all the various actions you need to take to reach your end game for each thing you conceive and for which you are asking. And if you aren't sure where to start, don't worry. I'll help you with that later in the book, too.

In short, this is the Mind-Morph Mechanism. Details of each element of the mechanism make up the chapters through the rest of the book.

Mind-Morph 101

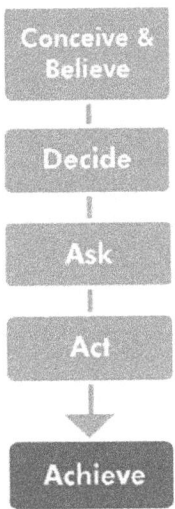

Because we live in reality, and not the Marvel Cinematic Universe® (dang it!), you will likely find you derail from the mechanism on occasion. Derailing is not uncommon. It happens to most of us. There are all sorts of reasons for it, and I cover a lot of them later in the book. To help you get back on track and stay true to the process, I include the <u>ABCs of the Mind-Morph Mechanism</u> as well. See what I did there? "<u>ABCs</u>" = keeping it simple. There is no need to overcomplicate a simple mechanism. I detail each aspect of the ABCs throughout the book. Follow the ABCs, and you will start to find more and more success in all aspects of your life – especially creating the ideal life you want for yourself!

The ABCs of the Mind-Morph Mechanism

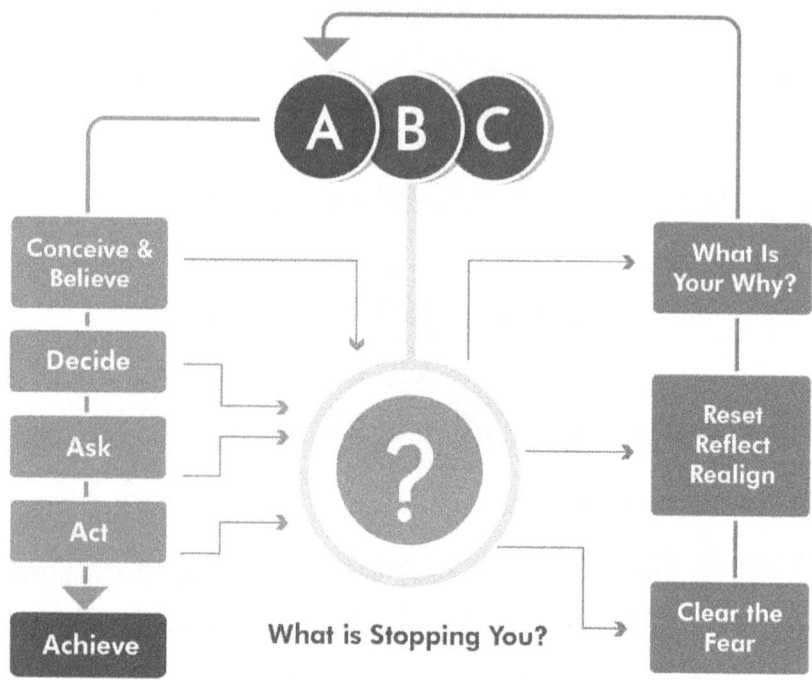

When you're living an "A" game all systems are go! Keep moving through the mechanism and repeat it for each new idea, challenge or life ideal you would like to achieve.

If you experience any sort of slow down during your journey (feel stuck, unsure, fearful, etc.) pause and ask yourself "What's stopping me?"

Consider the common elements in Section C to get back on track.

Most of what keeps us from achieving, falls into these three categories. Read through the chapter associated with your sticking point from Section A for some fresh perspective. Then go right back to where you left off and re-engage the mechanism to fulfill all you desire to achieve.

Copyright © Chris Doyle, Mind-Morph

CHAPTER 1

7 *Pretty Simple* Fundamentals to Change Your Life

"The most difficult thing is the decision to act. The rest is merely tenacity. The fears are paper tigers. You can do anything you decide to do. You can act to change and control your life and the procedure. The process is its own reward."

Amelia Earhart

I don't know about you, but I have been somewhat disappointed as I've read, studied, and applied various concepts and techniques in my attempt to improve any particular situation in my life. Inspirational phrases such as "Just Do It," "Ask, Believe, Receive," and "The Universe Will Deliver" seemed incomplete. They lack directions – the what, how and why. Just do what? How and who do I ask for something? When and how will the Universe deliver something to me?

You won't find any vague phrases or concepts thrown around here, sending you off into the world with the hope you are doing something "right" to achieve something which, in the end, may not be achievable at all. What you will find is a specific structure. Explanations behind every concept. Questions for you to answer which will help you consider where you are at this time in your life, and some action items that will start and keep you on the path to achieving those things most meaningful, most desirable and most achievable for YOU.

I said earlier that Mind-Morph is a change of mind. Change is a journey. I like to think of change as an *adventure*! Journeys and adventures, take time to complete. Even when change seems to occur quickly, there is an underlying journey that happens even though it may not be immediately apparent.

To understand, embrace, and apply the concepts throughout the book, you will embark upon a marvelous adventure. Like all good adventures, you will follow a plan, a course of action - a map, if you will. To follow a map, you have to know where you are starting. In Mind-Morph, your starting point is your Mind-Point. Changing your mind requires an awareness of your thinking as you begin the change.

Discovering your Mind-Point (your starting point) is to determine how much you may be living a Mind-Morph life already. You may find in some areas you are strong, while in other areas, you may be about average. You may want to focus a bit more on some areas than others. Remember, there is no good or bad here, only where you are and where you want to go. And, we'll be doing it together the whole way.

Now, this is going to seem like it's just a taste. And it is. With these 7 *Pretty Simple* Fundamentals to Change Your Life, we just discuss what each fundamental is and determine your Mind-Point. To get the juicy stuff and start putting it to work in your life, you have to read the whole book!

Are you ready? This is going to be an awesome ride!

Fundamental #1 – Can You Believe It?

One of my favorite people in history is President Theodore Roosevelt because he had an extremely powerful belief system. He had asthma as a child and was often sick. His mother would discourage him from being active and doing anything that required a lot of effort or physical exertion, although he loved the outdoors! At a young age, he'd already formed the character to embrace life and do the things he loved (regardless of how hard they might have seemed). He refused to become a victim of his illness. He went on to live an active lifestyle boxing and rowing in college and spending as much time outside as he possibly could.

> BELIEVE YOU CAN AND YOU'RE HALFWAY THERE.
>
> THEODORE ROOSEVELT

He'd made up his mind that he could accomplish anything he wanted. During the 1920s, a blizzard hit New York City, locking everything down. Despite the bad weather, he made the journey from his home across Manhattan to the New York Historical Society, where he was to attend a meeting. He became angry when he arrived, and no one else showed up. Some people might consider that stubbornness, and perhaps it was. It is also one of the contributing factors to why he would say, "If you believe you can, you're halfway there."

As individuals, our beliefs in nature, astrology, God, society, our friends, and families matter. However, what we believe about ourselves matters most.

Believing* is the first of these 7 Fundamentals. It is that important!

What you believe in (what your belief system "is") is not as important as **having** a belief system: "a set of principles or tenets which together form the basis of religion, philosophy or moral code." Whether you associate with a particular political party, have any religious foundation, honor a Higher Power or value the gifts of Mother Nature, all of these offer the significance of a support structure, a group of other like-minded people to associate and socialize with and the presence of possibility!

I would say it this way; belief systems support an understanding that things – all things – are possible. And as such, if you have a belief system, then all things are possible for you, as a believer within your system.

Let's begin to determine your Mind-Point for this adventure. At the end of each fundamental explained in the following pages, you are presented a brief survey similar to the one below.

Thoughtfully read each statement. Place a mark on the colored shape next to each statement, which most closely aligns with your point of view. When you complete the survey, tally your results.

*Please note shape colors only appear in the digital edition of the book.

▲ I COMPLETELY DISAGREE   ◆ I SOMEWHAT DISAGREE

● I SOMEWHAT AGREE   ■ I COMPLETELY AGREE

1) I believe in my ability to accomplish difficult tasks and overcome challenges.   ▲ ◆ ● ■

2) I believe in at least one other person (someone from history, a public figure, or someone from everyday life) who I admire and/or respect.   ▲ ◆ ● ■

3) I have a belief and support the concept of something (not someone) such as a cause, a movement, a philosophy, etc.   ▲ ◆ ● ■

4) I believe in a God or a Higher Power.   ▲ ◆ ● ■

5) I believe people can continue the process of learning and increasing in wisdom throughout their lifetimes.   ▲ ◆ ● ■

TOTAL RESULTS   ___ ___ ___ ___

Fundamental #2 – Buckets of Laws

If I were to ask you for the first thing that pops into your head when I say the word "law," you might cringe while you instantly recall that speeding ticket you received even if it was back when you were 16 years old! That's called an involuntary memory, and it happens because our brains keep the information and feelings associated with events like this to keep us from repeating them. Forming these connections is one of the most basic ways we learn, and it is important to the process of Mind-Morphing.

Ultimately, this process of linking memories and feelings sinks deep into the subconscious, and we don't even have to think about the act of doing; we do. If you've had the traumatic experience of getting a speeding ticket when you were first learning to drive, you probably never even think about whether or not you're speeding. You automatically stay fairly close to the speed limit.

In this book about changing your life, I chose a speeding ticket example for two reasons. 1) It is something we can all relate to – even if you've never had a negative speeding-ticket-getting experience. 2) It is also something that can be changed using the Mind-Morph Way, and I would bet a majority of readers would use the Mind-Morph mechanism for this reason alone!

Mind-Morph shows you that understanding and using all of

these laws together in a harmonious manner is what will set you up to live your most successful, most fulfilling, and most abundant life. The Mind-Morph Way teaches you the mechanism for creating your life, not just existing in it. That means reaching whatever levels of success, financial independence, social involvement, career direction, etc., you desire.

Law Bucket #1

Laws of Physics fall into the scientific category of general relativity (GR). They include things like the Law of Gravity, the Three Laws of Motion, and Einstein's theory of relativity, where he introduced the $E=mc^2$ formula. Outside the theories of Quantum Physics, we are all subject to them. Sir Isaac Newton studied and identified several physical laws which apply to large-mass items such as people and objects, all the way down to the atomic and sub-atomic level.

Law Bucket #2

Laws of Society are those which society, wherever you live, have defined as applicable to all people within the society. These are all those laws that apply while driving, plus all of the legal statutes which apply to various actions and activities within a society, such as opening or operating a business, building a home, etc.

Law Bucket #3

Laws of the Universe exist within the Universe (everything or all things). They are constant and consistent. Most people have heard of the Law of Attraction due to its recent popularity. However, it is just one of many. This Universal Law functions in a "like attract like" fashion. For example, if you are projecting positive energy (I call this "positive signaling"), the Universe returns positive energy to you. More about this later.

Law Bucket #4

Laws of the Spirit are those based on our individual spiritual beliefs or belief system principles, such as organized religion. Based on your spiritual beliefs and practices, these types of laws may include any of the Ten Commandments, i.e., Thou Shalt Not Steal, Thou Shalt Not Kill, as well as the Law of Tithing, or the Law of Reaping and Sowing. Whatever your personal spiritual beliefs or belief system, the laws that apply to your beliefs likely promote the power of positivity (or good), the realm of possibility, the opportunity to experience continual growth and development and, most importantly, a Higher Power you may be able to call upon for strength, support, and assistance. In fact, in his book *Think and Grow Rich*, Napoleon Hill refers to all of this as Infinite Intelligence. Some people believe in Mother Earth and others in spiritual deities or icons such as Buddha.

It is important to note that the Laws of the Spirit are guiding laws, interweaving among all other laws. You might consider the Laws of the Spirit to be the ultimate overseer of the laws within the other three law buckets.

> IT IS IMPORTANT TO NOTE THAT LAWS OF THE SPIRIT ARE THE HIGHEST LAWS AND TRANSCEND ALL OTHER LAWS.

7 *Pretty Simple* Fundamentals

Now, continue to determine your Mind-Point. Remember, as you consider each question, place a mark on the colored shape that matches your level of agreement about the statement as you consider your viewpoint today.

▲ I COMPLETELY DISAGREE   ◆ I SOMEWHAT DISAGREE
● I SOMEWHAT AGREE   ■ I COMPLETELY AGREE

1) I firmly believe in the existence of physical laws, such as the Law of Gravity. ▲ ◆ ● ■

2) I firmly believe in the laws of the society in which I live. I believe these laws to be for the betterment of all people. ▲ ◆ ● ■

3) I live the spiritual laws of my belief system. For example, if my belief system says to be kind to others, I live by that belief. ▲ ◆ ● ■

4) I believe in universal laws such as the Law of Attraction and the Law of Cause and Effect. ▲ ◆ ● ■

5) I believe that people are subject to those laws (in Question 4, above) even if their demonstrations are not visible or tangible. For example, if someone projects negative energy, they are subject to receiving negative energy. ▲ ◆ ● ■

TOTAL RESULTS _____ _____ _____ _____

Fundamental #3 – #FlipTheSwitch

When I was in high school, I caught my younger brother smoking. My mom smoked while we were growing up and had just quit about a year before when she married for the second time. My brother and I argued, and I'd told him I was going to tell mom he was smoking. His reply was, "Go ahead; she already knows." I was shocked!

Well, fast-forward five years. We were having lunch together, and I told my brother he needed to stop smoking. He said something along the lines of "I can quit any time I want." Another five years later, I told him again, and this time he said: "Yeah, I know I do, and I am going to make it a point to try." Five years later, he admitted, "Man, I have tried, and it is the hardest thing ever!" I have heard that from other people, too. Smoking may be one of the hardest habits to quit because it is an actual physical addiction. Your body becomes reliant on that nicotine "fix."

But, people do it. Some people even quit cold turkey – that's how my mom did it when she got re-married. As I've talked to hundreds of people over the years, I've discovered one common thread when it comes to quitting smoking, and I think it applies to all aspects of quitting OR starting something. That is, the actual process of *deciding* to do it. As I've gotten to the root of the problem with people who are struggling to quit, I often hear something along the lines of "the truth is, I don't WANT to quit." Many people, quite honorably, want to quit for great reasons – for their loved ones, for better health, to save money by not buying cigarettes, etc. However, when it comes down to it, deep inside, they haven't flipped that switch – they haven't decided they want it for themselves.

The success stories I've heard, and been a part of, go something like this – "I just decided I was doing it, and that was it." For my mom, she wanted to please her new husband more than anything else. That was the trigger that caused her to make the conscious and sub-conscious decision she didn't need to smoke any more. I'm not saying she didn't feel the effects of smoking withdrawal. However, she made it through because she made a firm decision not to smoke.

> SETTING A GOAL IS NOT THE MAIN THING. IT IS DECIDING TO DO IT.

That's what flipping the switch is when you Mind-Morph. It's kind of like reaching way back into your brain and turning a light switch up or down. Whether you want to *stop* something – like smoking, aggressive driving, not yelling at your kids, or to *start* something – like beginning a new career, committing to a relationship, or treating your employees better – you have to decide you are going to do it genuinely! Keep reading to see how to put your decision into action.

Ok, it's Mind-Point time again. Check yourself and see how you feel about where you are when it comes to flipping the switch.

▲ I COMPLETELY DISAGREE   ◆ I SOMEWHAT DISAGREE
● I SOMEWHAT AGREE   ■ I COMPLETELY AGREE

1) When it comes to deciding, I usually make a decision and stick with it.   ▲ ◆ ● ■

2) It is not difficult for me to make life-changing decisions such as a career change or moving to another state.   ▲ ◆ ● ■

3) Before I make a decision, I take the time to understand why I'm making the choice I am.   ▲ ◆ ● ■

4) I've struggled with following through after I've made a decision, such as losing weight, quitting smoking, or something similar.   ▲ ◆ ● ■

5) I feel like I have pretty strong will power.   ▲ ◆ ● ■

TOTAL RESULTS _____   _____   _____   _____

Fundamental #4 – Ready, Set, Get

I have traveled most of my professional career. As an entrepreneur in the IT and Telecom industries, I literally "went to where the money was." In other words, I had to place myself in the client locations to earn my keep. Even when I was a paid employee, my roles required attendance at customer sites across the country, tradeshows, conferences, and engineering meetings at various company facilities around the world.

The first time I traveled to Japan, I wanted to make a positive impression as part of a global team and had my mind set on introducing myself in Japanese as best I could. My Japanese mentor wrote out my introduction in Japanese, and I rehearsed it over and over on the 12-hour flight. One other thing I learned to say was Tasukete! (tah-sue-keh-tay) – meaning *Help!* My mentor and other colleagues always made sure I had what I needed and also wanted to make sure I knew how to ask for help.

It's interesting. If we need help, we must go through the physical process of *asking* for it. Sometimes we might even have to seek out someone to help with particular needs. If we fall into some medical distress in the grocery store or while eating at a restaurant, people may run to our aid. Although they might not help us until we ask for it by saying the word "help." One perceived challenge in asking for help is the vulnerability our request creates for us. Because most people don't like the feeling of vulnerability, unless we are in a life-threatening situation, we have trouble asking for help. The extra problem with all of this is the uneasy feeling of vulnerability when asking for help that translates to an uneasy feeling when asking for anything. Some of us don't even like to ask for directions!

You will discover, as you immerse yourself deeper into these fundamentals, Mind-Morph sets *you* – your conscious and subconscious self – into harmonious alignment. Alignment with the natural order of laws and the energies of the Universe to create, and live, the fulfilled life you most desire. Please understand this concept, and the mechanism engaged in achieving it is not new. It's been around since the beginning of time, and its use is well known. And, it all starts with the "ask." More about that later.

As we continue to gather information to determine your Mind-Point, see where you feel like you measure out when it comes to asking.

> IF YOU DON'T ASK, YOU DON'T GET.
>
> STEVIE WONDER

7 *Pretty Simple* Fundamentals

 I COMPLETELY DISAGREE   I SOMEWHAT DISAGREE

 I SOMEWHAT AGREE   I COMPLETELY AGREE

1) I find it easy to ask others for help if it is an emergency or if I am in a desperate situation.   ▲ ◆ ● ■

2) I find it easy to ask others for help in any situation where help is needed.   ▲ ◆ ● ■

3) I turn to God (or my Higher Power) and ask for help, guidance, direction, blessings, etc.   ▲ ◆ ● ■

4) When I turn to others and ask for help, in any situation, I fully expect to receive help.   ▲ ◆ ● ■

5) When I turn to God and ask for help, in any situation, I fully expect to receive help.   ▲ ◆ ● ■

TOTAL RESULTS

Fundamental #5 – "Action" Isn't a Noun

When I facilitate leadership development programs, I have the opportunity to help my participants understand the ways they are naturally, internally wired. Many of us have various behaviors, and either don't realize we have them or, if we do, we aren't sure why. One example of a characteristic many people possess is a lack of assertiveness. When someone is less assertive, it's apparent by what that person doesn't do: avoiding confrontation of any type, not speaking up in meetings, and not proactively presenting their perspective or opinions.

As I spend quality one-on-one time with these leaders of every type and position, I have the opportunity to discover that many of them have tremendously good ideas. They have ideas of all shapes and sizes. Some would certainly save their company money or streamline a process. Some ideas are related to their church or community. Others for inventions and some innovative business concepts. However, none of what's inside these brilliant brains ever makes it out into worldly existence partly due

> ACTION IS WHAT TURNS HUMAN DREAMS INTO SIGNIFICANCE.
>
> JOHN C. MAXWELL

to the natural tendency to be less assertive – to avoid taking action. Can you imagine the gains, across all types of business, industry, education, and every different area we would see in this world if only everyone would take action on the ideas and concepts they can conceive?

American actress Gillian Anderson said, "Just remember, you can do anything you set your mind to, but it takes action, perseverance, and facing your fears." I have great news for those of you who feel you are less assertive or have fears that may be holding you back from the action it takes to reach your ideal life: You can change your thinking using Mind-Morph. I can help you get started even if you have no idea where to start!

Mind-Morph

So, Morph on and determine your Mind-Point for taking action. Remember, place a mark on the colored shape that matches your level of agreement about the statement.

▲ I COMPLETELY DISAGREE   ◆ I SOMEWHAT DISAGREE

● I SOMEWHAT AGREE   ■ I COMPLETELY AGREE

1) I feel like I take action on my ideas and concepts most of the time.   ▲ ◆ ● ■

2) I have no problem expressing my opinions in a group or work-related meetings.   ▲ ◆ ● ■

3) My family and friends would say that I am a self-starter.   ▲ ◆ ● ■

4) I prefer to take action rather than reacting to events.   ▲ ◆ ● ■

5) I would rather act on something with a risk of failure than not to act at all.   ▲ ◆ ● ■

TOTAL RESULTS ____ ____ ____ ____

Fundamental #6 – Reflect, Reset, Realign

Since you're reading this book, chances are you've been through some rough patches in life. I have as well – raised by a single parent at the poverty level until I was 18, two divorces, bankruptcy, repossession. You name it, and I've likely endured it. The tie that binds us is not the similarities in our past. It is the fact that we're survivors. We're still here and still pressing ever forward. Surviving our past challenges doesn't mean we're done working. We're facing new challenges all the time – every day.

There was a period in my life when it seemed like *nothing* was going right. Not only was nothing going right, it also seemed like everything I touched turned to stone. Even things that had absolutely no reason to go wrong were going wrong. It all drove me into a down and depressed headspace, which seemed impossible to escape. In the midst of all this, I was asked to start assisting an elderly gentleman who attended our church. Not only was he elderly, he was also one of those guys who always seemed to be in a terrible mood. And he took it out on everyone else around him. I remember thinking, "This is not going to go well at all!"

I buckled down and scheduled a visit with him. I prayed the entire drive, asking God and the Universe to send me as much support and positive energy as possible. I arrived, greeted by a warm and friendly smile from a person who was not at all the crotchety man I'd seen at church. I was stunned. We had a wonderful talk with each other that day. On other afternoons, we worked on small projects around his apartment, discussing what was happening in the world, or I listened to him play beautifully on his small, electronic keyboard. Not only had I quickly endeared myself to him, I also found myself being grateful for everything I had in my life. I was grateful I had car problems because it meant I had a car. I was grateful my kids' extracurricular activity schedule conflicted with my work schedule because it meant I had the blessing of being surrounded by great kids! I was starting to see things from a different perspective. And, while my situation hadn't changed that much, my outlook had changed a lot. What previously felt bad, negative, and "against me" was looking better and even hinted at being for my good.

> WHEN YOU START LIVING THE MIND-MORPH WAY, YOU'LL LIKELY HAVE SOME SETBACKS.

When I look back on this situation and others like it, I can see (in hindsight) the purpose and the perfection in all things. I can see how going through this experience realigned my thoughts and my position within the state of things to bring me back to the center. Understanding the perfection in things can be a hard philosophy to adopt amid a chaotic life. However, it is one that you will want to embrace.

When you start living the Mind-Morph Way, you'll likely have some setbacks (which are set<u>ups</u> for your next good thing). Although you'll be able to move through setbacks in a much better way than you do now. You will also recognize them as learning opportunities and treat them as positive events rather than negative events. You'll also have some tools you can use to reframe where you are at the time, regroup and get yourself back into positive, forward-facing momentum.

Mind-Point time once again. Take a deeper, more meaningful look at how satisfied you are with how you manage the tough times. The more honest you are with yourself here, the easier it will be to incorporate the Mind-Morph Way to achieve your results.

▲ I COMPLETELY DISAGREE   ◆ I SOMEWHAT DISAGREE

● I SOMEWHAT AGREE   ■ I COMPLETELY AGREE

1) Right now, where I am today, I feel as though I am living in a positive space with little negativity around me.   ▲ ◆ ● ■

2) When I have minor struggles at work, or outside my home life, I can work through them easily.   ▲ ◆ ● ■

3) When I have minor struggles in my home life, I can work through them easily.   ▲ ◆ ● ■

4) If I have a major challenge of any type, i.e., loss of a job, divorce, etc., I feel I can manage through the situation on my own with little outside support.   ▲ ◆ ● ■

5) If I have a major challenge of any type, I usually try and find the purpose in such things and view these events from a more positive position.   ▲ ◆ ● ■

TOTAL RESULTS   ____ ____ ____ ____

Fundamental #7 – A Key to The Universe

Before we start talking about the key to the Universe, let's take a quick look at the previous six fundamentals and what we've determined on your Mind-Point.

1) **Believe** – It's important to *understand* what your belief system is (not important "what" the belief system is). As you will learn, the Mind-Morph Way embraces all people of all beliefs. Understanding your beliefs is an important part.

2) **Laws** – I would also add "order" to laws. Embracing the concept that everything (the world, nature, the Universe, "all of it") operates in an orderly fashion and abides by laws within its respective system. If you want to understand how something works, look into the set of laws it operates within.

3) **Decide** – You need to decide, sincerely decide you want and are ready for those things you ask for, AND that you are ready to ASK, and ACT, in order to: *create the abundant life you desire, attract those things in life you want or need and become the person who embodies this constant state of being.*

4) **Ask** – The Universe will deliver what you ask for – consciously and subconsciously, positive or negative,

good for you or bad for you. It feeds the energy it receives from you right back to you. Being certain about what you are asking for, being positive about it, and getting to a point where you are projecting that *ask* at the subconscious level is living the Mind-Morph Way.

5) **Act** – There are several universal laws, and one of them is the Law of Action. After asking for something, you still need to put a plan into motion to obtain it. You must ACT for Mind-Morph to work correctly.

6) **Realign** – If and when you are out of alignment with any part of the Mind-Morph mechanism, it will be important to realign. To get back on track, reground, regroup, re-center yourself. It's similar to balancing on a balance beam and walking heel-to-toe from one end to another. As soon as you lose your balance and start to fall, you immediately reposition yourself upright and on sure footing as you continue to the other side.

And now for being a key to the Universe. As you can probably tell, Mind-Morph is taking you from where you are now to where you want to be. There are no limits or boundaries in any part of this mechanism. As Napoleon Hill said, "Whatever the mind of man can conceive and believe, it can achieve." The Mind-Morph Way will show you how to live in a conceive-believe-achieve manner on a daily basis consciously. Mind-Morph turns **YOU** into the **KEY** that unlocks the Universe.

Imagine one of those wooden Chinese three-dimensional brain teaser toys. They come completely unsolved with only a single piece of paper showing what the toy looks like when it is solved. These puzzles seem impossible. I have even thought to myself; there is no way these pieces of wood can be assembled in any fashion to look like that picture! When I think that way, I've pretty much already defeated myself. There is a way. There is always a solution. There may be only a single solution, however there is a solution, a *key* to making it work.

> YOU'VE BEEN IN HARMONIOUS ALIGNMENT AT LEAST ONCE, AND FOR SOME, MAYBE EVEN MORE THAN THAT!

Now imagine yourself and everything that embodies you and your life – job, family, friends, experiences, beliefs, values, everything. The goal, the achievement, or the ideal life is the puzzle. The solution to everything you want in life is merely a matter of situating yourself in the form that makes it work. *You are the **key**.* You situate the perfect alignment with the Universe and all of the energies, events, and activities needed for you to create the solution. And there are two guarantees I can make to every reader – First, you've been in harmonious alignment at least once in your life. That's right! You've already done it at least once, and maybe even more than that. Think back to any time when it seemed like all things were as they should be – they were perfect for that moment. That is when you were in alignment. You were the *key* that turned the lock on the Universe and opened the door to all things. Second – just like the Chinese puzzle, when you know the solution, it's not impossible anymore. When you figure out the solution to the puzzle, you probably go around to all your friends and tell them to try and solve it. If they can't, you easily do it in front of them so they can see the solution. You do it over and over for anyone who will watch. The same is true for your own life. Once you figure out how you can make the Universe work for you, you will start to do it more and more, over and over, and you will consistently create and attract the things you want in life.

Let's finish out your Mind-Point.

 I COMPLETELY DISAGREE   I SOMEWHAT DISAGREE

 I SOMEWHAT AGREE   I COMPLETELY AGREE

1) I believe in the existence of a universal connection or energy among people and things.

2) I have had the experience of projecting positive energy into the world (in any capacity) and receiving positive energy back.

3) I believe in Karma, i.e., what goes around, comes around.

4) I think there are some things about the world, nature and Universe we, as people, don't know.

5) I feel like I am mentally and emotionally stronger when I have positive people around me.

TOTAL RESULTS ——— ——— ——— ———

And just like that, you've concluded the 7 *Pretty Simple* Fundamentals to Change Your Life. And they are pretty simple, don't you agree? There might be one or two fundamentals that give you a challenge at first. However, I know you can meet that challenge head-on to create positive change in your life.

What's your Starting Point?

To determine your Mind-Point, add up the total results for each survey. Enter your grand totals for each colored shape here:

_____   _____   _____   _____

The colored shape with the highest number is where you tend to land most naturally. Again, there is no right or wrong here. No judgment about your level. It is only a picture of where you are, compared to where you would like to be. *It is your starting point for your change of mind.*

If you are a **Triangle**, it could indicate you possess an internal tendency to want to see concrete examples, firm proof, a need to experience something personally vs. believing it due to someone else's experience, or an "I'll believe it when I see it" perspective.

A stronger **Diamond** may mean you're more of a follower of someone else's leadership. You will probably believe something if someone you trust and value tells you a certain thing is true or has a strong belief, and you might be more willing to adopt the beliefs and follow the group or team.

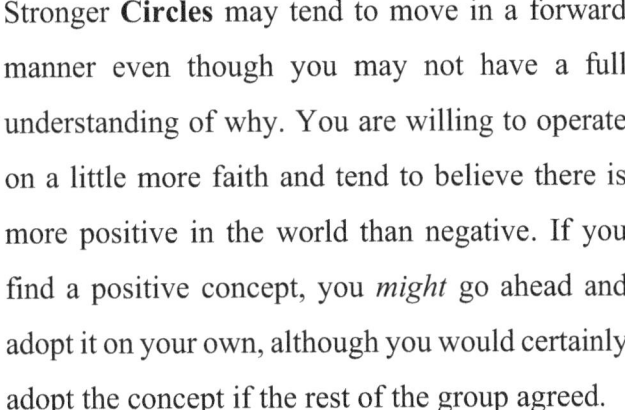Stronger **Circles** may tend to move in a forward manner even though you may not have a full understanding of why. You are willing to operate on a little more faith and tend to believe there is more positive in the world than negative. If you find a positive concept, you *might* go ahead and adopt it on your own, although you would certainly adopt the concept if the rest of the group agreed.

If you are a stronger **Square**, you have likely had positive experiences throughout life and may have even had a positive role model and/or mentor (or two). You may lean towards win-win scenarios, giving people the benefit of the doubt and operate from the "glass is half full" perspective.

If you have scores that might be close together, say a close Triangle and Diamond or Diamond and Circle, etc. it only means your life experiences and conditioning have led you in both of those shape directions. For example, it is not at all uncommon for someone to be a strong Triangle and equally strong Square. The general outlook of that person may be that they need more concrete proof that something is true. They may also have had a positive role model who influenced them that concrete proof is necessary when formulating beliefs.

Once again, there is no right or wrong, and you should consider your Mind-Point to be a litmus test for the starting point of your Mind-Morph experience. You may want to reflect and consider whether any of your answers struck a particular chord with you or even how you felt while answering the questions. That's where the real work comes in. If you experienced an "ah-ha" moment where you thought you would score one way, and you scored differently, that, in and of itself, is a GREAT point of awareness.

> WHEN YOU CHANGE WHAT YOU THINK, YOU CHANGE WHAT YOU CAN DO.
>
> NAPOLEON HILL

CHAPTER 2

Can You Believe It?

"And all things, whatsoever ye shall ask in prayer, believing, ye shall receive."
Matthew 21:22

Beliefs

Everything in our lives starts with beliefs. As humans, we *believe* what we *think*, and we can completely think ourselves into **any** particular belief. That word "any" can be positive or negative, and here's one of the reasons it works that way. What you *think* ultimately becomes what you *do*. And not just what you do once or twice. It becomes what you do all the time – your habits.

There are various versions of what I refer to as the "WATCH expression," which go back to the mid-1800s, and that expression goes like this:

Watch your thoughts; they become words;
watch your words; they become actions;
watch your actions; they become habits;
watch your habits; they become character;
watch your character, for it becomes your destiny.

Beliefs ➔ Actions ➔ Habits = Who You Are

Thought and the state of believing is a wonderfully powerful process. I do mean to say "power." It works with equal strength positively or negatively in our lives. Think of the gas pedal in your car. The engine receives the gas, and the car moves. It doesn't matter if you are going forward or backward or if you are running into something. The gas provides power equally.

Consider how quickly we think ourselves out of various situations or adopt limiting beliefs. A limiting belief is any belief (or thought) that holds us back or keeps us from doing something. Often these beliefs have no real basis, although we treat them as factual. Before we've even had time to consider a new option, we are already thinking ourselves out of it.

Limiting vs. Non-Limiting Beliefs

One challenge we face when making a significant change in our life (or way of thinking) is to flip *limiting* beliefs, thoughts and behaviors to **non-limiting** beliefs, thoughts and behaviors.

For example, for people who are struggling with weight loss, some limiting beliefs may be:

- I'm too overweight for dieting to work.
- I'm too overweight to exercise.

- I can't lose weight because obesity runs in my family.
- Nothing will work.

Non-limiting beliefs you can adopt in place of these might be:
- I can lose weight by committing to a diet plan.
- I can reach my desired weight by working out with a trainer.
- Obesity seems to run in my family, however, I will find a way to overcome it.
- There is something that will work for me, and I will keep looking until I find it.

Conditioning

As you reason through the notion that your thoughts become your destiny, consider how thoughts first turn into habits and later into firmly-planted beliefs.

How did you come to adopt the beliefs and belief system you have today? More than likely, repetition was involved. Perhaps one of your beliefs (positive or negative) is something you've heard over and over from someone, which eventually you began to tell yourself over and over. That constant hearing and/or telling yourself is so deeply embedded it becomes your truth – your belief. Even if your *truth* isn't true at all.

So why do we do it? Why do we narrow or restrict our thinking, limiting our beliefs, and thereby limiting our achievements in life? Well, I have some bad news and some good news as to how we come to believe what we do. The bad news is that our beliefs are a direct result of our conditioning. Conditioning is your experience from the time your brain starts processing information to this moment. It is all of your experiences, everything you've learned, everything you've been exposed to in life – especially any experience which had a deeper impact on you than others. For example, if you grew up in a household where any verbal, physical or mental abuse occurred, then those experiences formed the basis of your beliefs today. These beliefs may manifest themselves in a lack of trust in others or trying to protect yourself by avoiding serious relationships.

> THE GREAT NEWS IS – YOU CAN BE CONDITIONED OUT OF A LIMITING BELIEF!

I can be a pretty skeptical person. I've learned that my skepticism is part of my internal wiring – my belief system. I'm sure there are many reasons for my tendency to look more critically at things at first, but let's say it is a result of my conditioning.

Here's the GREAT news! Since you have been, and continue to be, conditioned into beliefs, you can condition yourself out of beliefs. Let me say that again, a little differently: You can condition yourself into *new* beliefs. The process of reconditioning may not always be easy. However, it is entirely possible. People do it every day. Remember what you believe to be *important* because you will act (that is also to say you will ***live***) based on what you believe is true and **possible**. And, it is critical to your growth as you live the Mind-Morph Way.

Misbeliefs

Misbeliefs may at first seem to be the same as fears. However, misbeliefs are fears we've embedded into our belief system and registered as truths. Sometimes we short-circuit possibilities with what *appears* to be reasonable explanations. As it turns out, those explanations are just excuses, the "story" we tell ourselves, limiting beliefs – or misbeliefs – about what the opportunity realistically is.

There does need to be a rationale in what we are asking – for example, many talented singers audition for the *American Idol* television show. Unfortunately, there are many singers lacking talent who audition as well. It wouldn't be the Mind-Morph Way to say the singers lacking talent can never be big stars. That is completely counter-intuitive to what Mind-Morph represents. Some of the less talented singers might need voice coaching; they may need to change their appearance; they may need to choose different song titles. There is a myriad of legitimate reasons these singers don't make it on the show. However, one misbelief may be that they "aren't what the judges are looking for," "they are too 'edgy' for prime time," or the judges "don't like me." These are their stories or excuses.

As students of Mind-Morph, these individuals would establish what it is they deeply want. Do they want to be on the show? Do they want to get a record contract? Or, do they want to be the next Pop Music superstar? Then, they would strongly consider WHY they want what they have decided. If the why is superficial or material, such as a "lot of money and fame," their Higher Power, and subsequently the Universe, may not deliver.

If what they want and why they want it is more heartfelt and more meaningful, then maybe the results look different. In this example, let's say a participant does not make it on the show. Her *want* is to perform well enough to sign with a record label. Her *why* is because she is an advocate for underprivileged children, and she would like to bring music and enjoyment to impoverished areas. This person, asking for all things she needs to succeed in this desire, might quickly be introduced to a voice coach, who then introduces her to a manager, who then introduces her to a record label. Before you know it, she realized her dream – not in the way she might first have expected, which was winning on *American Idol*. If she would have held on to a misbelief, she might have otherwise given up quickly, and never realized a real dream. How many of us have done this in our lives?

Consider what some of your misbeliefs might be for the goal you want to achieve:

- Do you think you are too old?
- How about too young?
- Do you feel like you don't have the money it takes?
- Is your excuse you don't have the talent or the knowledge or the skill?
- Are you too heavy? Or not big enough?
- Are you too busy?

The Science

I like to be able to understand the *why* behind the views I adopt. It's no different with this concept of belief. Like you, I want to understand *why* it is important that I believe in certain things. As it turns out, this is a pretty natural way of thinking for most of us. We like it when we think like other people, and we like it more when we find some sort of *proof* that our way of thinking is **right**. However, we also have to be careful of proving false points.

Heck! If someone wants to find some evidence of something, regardless of how inaccurate it may be, that person can probably do it with a quick search of the Internet.

The Placebo Effect

The science of believing – and, more importantly, changing our beliefs for the better – is full of encouraging and reliable documentation. In the book *The Healing Brain*, by Robert Evan Ornstein and David Sobel, the authors describe the effects on the brain and the body through the combination of the power of suggestion and placebo (a fake treatment, such as a pill or shot, used more for a psychological effect rather than a physiological effect). For example, a patient complained of nausea. All medical tests administered verified she was experiencing the physical symptoms of nausea. She was given medicine (which was a placebo) and told by the doctor that she is receiving the most powerful solution for nausea known at the time. After taking medicine, not only did the patient stop *thinking* she had nausea (the brain part), she was also no longer indicating the physical signs of nausea (the body part).

How the Brain Works

That powerful experiment shows how significantly we control our minds (and control our bodies with our minds), especially under circumstances that have deeper, more meaningful impact. In this case, the patient was working with a doctor – a title she respects and trusts. What she believed changed somewhat quickly. Under the circumstances outside of this type of study, though, while the change in beliefs still does happen, it may not occur at this particular rate and pace. Here's why:

Art Markman, Ph.D., professor of Psychology and Marketing at the University of Texas at Austin, has written about research indicating firmly regarded beliefs interconnect to other similar concepts within our belief system. Here's what that essentially means in a real-life example about me:

- Chris drives fast.
  - Chris likes to drive fast because it's FUN!
    - Chris thinks driving fast is fun because he's had enjoyable, positive experiences driving fast cars.
    - He believes when he is driving fast, he remains a safe driver.
  - Chris has the mental capacity to move at a quick pace.
    - He thrives in business environments where quick thinking and working is required. He performs well in those situations and receives good pay and positive feedback

from his peers.
- He appreciates the expression "the shortest distance between two points is a straight line" because it generally describes the quickest way to get somewhere or accomplish some task.

➢ Chris has a firm belief that one particular route from his house to the local grocery store is the BEST route to take.

Now, if another person in the family (who shall remain nameless to protect the innocent) tries to tell Chris the other, second route to the store is faster, he will not believe that person. He believes that his route is the best. Even if he receives some evidence showing that the other route may be better, it will still be hard for him to change his belief that his chosen route is the best. It will be hard to change due to other beliefs within his system – he is a safe driver, he loves driving fast, he appreciates taking the shortest path – which holds him back from believing that anything except for *his belief* is best.

The effort to change is even harder when it is associated with the habit. The brain stores habits in the basal ganglia – this is where something goes when it becomes routine, such as driving a particular route to the grocery store. However, the decision-making process occurs in a part of the brain called the prefrontal cortex. To start to break the habit, you have to be able to intercept a thought at the prefrontal cortex and make a new/different decision.

Managing Beliefs

For Chris to be convinced another route to the store is better, he would have to be willing to allow himself to open his mind and thoughts to the opportunity that there *could be* a better, faster way than the one he has adopted. ***He has to believe in the <u>possibility</u> of something better.*** Let me repeat that – to grow in the Mind-Morph Way, you need to believe in the <u>*possibility*</u> of things. That it is, in fact, possible for you to attain anything you desire in any capacity. For me, this would mean being open to the idea that I could still get to the destination by driving in the manner I like and save time while doing it. Then, and only then, would I be able to start to change my mind, and my belief, by accepting the possibility of a better way.

> WE MUST START WITH THE BELIEF IN THE POSSIBILITY OF SOMETHING BETTER.

It is opening our minds to new possibilities before we can see them. When we think of the whole process in these terms, it can be somewhat mystifying as to how any of us change our minds and beliefs about anything. Seriously! On the surface, it seems as challenging as trying to learn a foreign language simply by moving to a new country. Here's the cool thing: since the science of thought has figured this out and tells how it works, we now know how to alter our thought system and make it work more as we want it.

How to Change Beliefs

Here are three points you can observe and implement for adopting new beliefs, which bring you closer to obtaining those things you desire.

Beliefs You Have
1) Determine which belief(s) may have held you back from an achievement or goal in your past. When identifying these limiting beliefs, it may help to think about times you made statements or had thoughts that started with any form of:

    "I can't…,"

    "I'm not…,"

    "There's no way…,"

    "It will never…,"

    Sentences with these phrases are often limiting beliefs.

Beliefs You Want

2) Determine what you want to believe in those situations you've identified that were previously limiting. What new beliefs will replace the old, limiting ones? In other words, what is your new belief that would change your previous statements and thoughts into "I can...," "I am...," "This is the way...," "It will..." and so on?

Action Steps

3) Determine the best techniques to remind yourself of your new approach and support your new, NON-LIMITING beliefs in those things you choose.

Some techniques which may keep these new beliefs at the front and center of your daily life might include:

- Write a positive note reminding yourself of your new belief, such as "I will energetically embrace losing 20 pounds!" and placing it in areas where you will see it often and throughout the day. A computer monitor, the refrigerator or the bathroom mirror are great places to start.
- Have daily conversations with people supporting your efforts. This support network could include close, positive-minded friends, support groups, and even

family members who may also share your motivations.

- Commit to your new belief with positive actions. If you desire better health, for example, go to a weight loss center, fitness center, or nutritionist.

Your Mind-Point

It's time to get into an exercise where you can apply the belief fundamental. Before we do, let's check in on your Mind-Point to increase your understanding of your natural wiring as you begin to change your beliefs.

As a **Triangle**, you may find it a challenge to begin changing a belief. There may be many reasons you feel it's a struggle. One will almost certainly be the need for proof the process works or a strong desire to experience positive results before committing. Don't give up too easily. You are aware of this characteristic, and you know it is part of your nature. Allow yourself to let go of this "need," this "belief," so you can achieve a positive outcome.

Diamonds find it easier to begin changing your beliefs if you have someone doing it with you – an "accountability partner." Or if you know of someone who has already done it. As with Triangles, My invitation is to let go of the limiting belief that you must see it work, for soon, you will see the *results for yourself.*

For **Circles**, you may be a bit hesitant at first. For the most part, you are ready and willing to look at where you can begin to believe in stronger and better possibilities about yourself and the opportunities ahead of you. You, too, will see faster results if you can flip limiting beliefs, causing you hesitancy to non-limiting beliefs, i.e., "I know I can!"

The **Square** group will be much more willing to "live and let live" as it's said, and readily begin the process of looking inward to examine your limiting beliefs. Your natural optimism may tempt you to label a limiting belief as *non-limiting*. If you recognize your limiting beliefs honestly, you are certain to find success!

Take some time to think about your beliefs, how you feel about the belief system you live within from day-to-day, and how those beliefs may be hindering you from living/creating a fulfilled life. When are you using phrases such as "I never," "I always," "It's not possible," etc.? How can you change those phrases to a positive form? Change these thoughts and, therefore your beliefs, to change your actions and your life!

Changed Beliefs → Changed Actions → Changed Habits = The NEW You

Write out the beliefs you currently have which you feel *might keep you from* contributing to the achievement of your Morph-Star:

_____
_____
_____

Write out the beliefs you currently have which you feel *will contribute to* the achievement of your Morph-Star:

_____
_____
_____

Write out the beliefs you do not currently have which you would *most like to adopt* in order to reach the advances in life you most desire:

_____
_____
_____

Write out at *least three (3) actions* you can take which will remind you to create a new habit of thinking in order to adopt those new beliefs you've identified above:

_____

_____

_____

At this point you are getting into the habit of changing your thoughts. You're creating a stronger belief system surrounding newly adopted beliefs, transforming your life into the life you most desire. Believing isn't the only principle needed for changing your life. If it were, this would be a short book!

You can't experience anything of significance by belief alone. You are putting positive energy and action into making changes – starting with changing how and what you believe. You will continue this pattern of believing and acting to reach heights far greater than you might have first imagined.

> A MAN IS BUT THE PRODUCT OF HIS THOUGHTS – WHAT HE THINKS, HE BECOMES.
>
> MAHATMA GANDHI

A True Story of Belief

So far, we've focused primarily on your personal beliefs. Certainly, some of those may be part of a bigger, external belief system such as a religion, a community, or even a belief system within your workplace (considered "work culture").

Allow me to emphasize the importance of actively taking part in a wider belief system. The support from others, positive influences, motivation, learning and acceptance from within the system are all factors that will help you begin to achieve at higher levels. By design, the wider system fosters the growth of each of its contributors, which in turn promotes the growth of the system. This phenomenon creates an organic, universal win-win for the individual, as well as the system. That win-win, as you will come to learn from Mind-Morph, is the ultimate delivery method for all the things you want in life.

One of many true examples starts with a little boy at age 10. There is almost nothing notable or significant about him. He and his family are one of many in the sea of a welfare system in the mid-1970s. Single mom, three kids, living at the poverty level with no child support (and no "Deadbeat Dad" laws at the time). This family lives on a minimum wage of $2.10 an hour, food stamps, free lunches, clothes from the only consignment shop in town, and the occasional donation from a friend or neighbor. With no other family nearby, the one thing they do have is each other.

Mom and dad were stereotypical products of the 1960s. Dad is backpacking around the country while mom raises the kids. Both "enjoyed" the era of "Peace, Love and Rock and Roll" to its fullest extent. As you picture this little boy in his living room, imagine a marijuana plant growing in a carefully placed pot in the corner. The 10-year-old received stern instructions not to let his younger brother or sister near that plant. As the man of the house, the protection of the plant is one of the many responsibilities he now owns.

If this young boy, or his siblings, were to grow into minimum-wage-earning, welfare-needing, drug-using adults, I don't think one person who knows the family would ever question why. A failed life is exactly the future for these kids.

Until one day, while playing in the vacant lot next door to the housing projects where he lives, the boy is met by two pretty, well-dressed young ladies in their late teens.

> WITH A LITTLE WORK, AND SOME HELP FROM GOD, YOU CAN DO OR BE ANYTHING YOU WANT.

They begin to talk to him and show him a kindness he does not often experience outside his family. They ask him if he knows about God. He tells them he does. They ask if he would like to come to their church on Sunday, and the boy agrees.

He hesitantly boards the church bus the next Sunday, and it seems to get easier each time he does. As he attends that church over the next several months, he learns about God and makes new friends. His Sunday School teacher, and others, ask what he wants in life. What does he want to do or be? He says what I think a lot of 10-year-olds would say: "I want to drive a race car," or "I want to play music," or "I like building things."

"You can do any of that," he is told. "With a little work and some help from God, you can do or be anything you want." And, his beliefs began to take hold and shape the person he would eventually become.

To be continued...

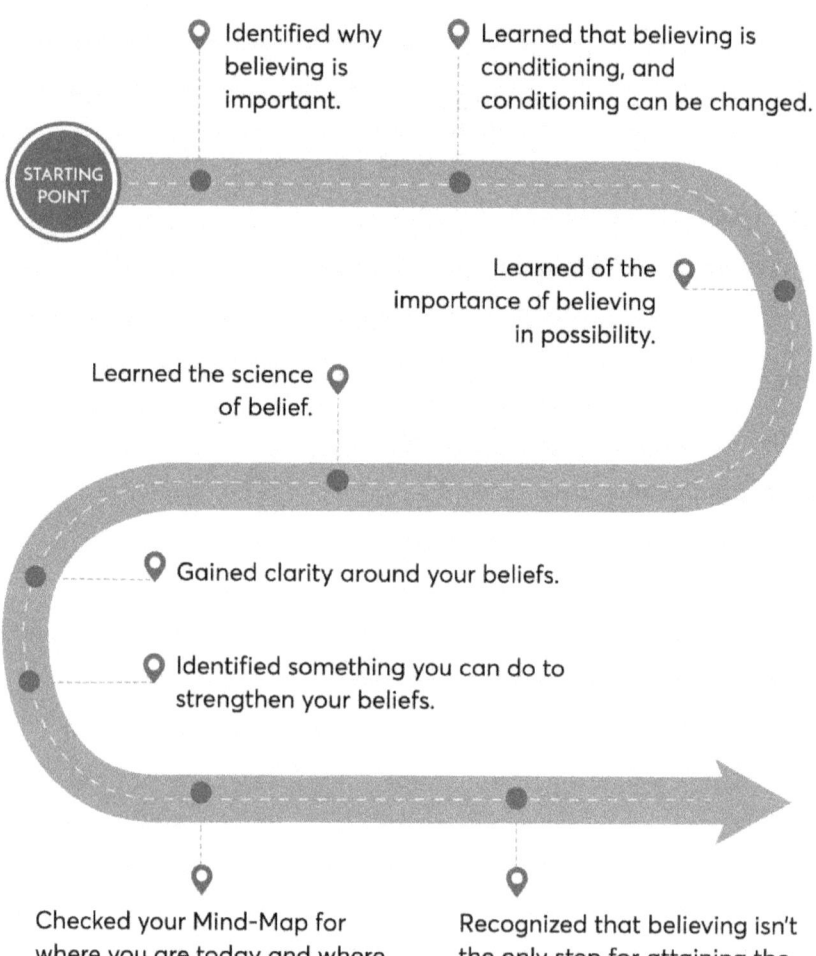

Copyright © Chris Doyle, Mind-Morph

Chapter 3
Buckets of Laws

"Gravity must be caused by an Agent acting constantly according to certain laws, but whether the Agent be material or immaterial I have left to the consideration of my readers."
Isaac Newton

Most people understand there is an order to things. For example, the sun rises and sets every 24 hours. The way the earth rotates and how it revolves around the sun stimulates other natural orders, such as seasons. Spring always precedes Summer. Summer precedes Fall, and Fall precedes Winter. Always. Society accepts these *truths*.

Certain laws are the basis of these truths. Gravity is probably the easiest to understand and the most familiar. The Law of Gravity stipulates there is a constant force pulling all objects toward the ground. Therefore, what goes up must come down. Even Isaac Newton conceded, however, the ultimate source of gravitational force is for us to determine. We know gravity is a result of the spinning of the earth. What force causes the earth to spin? What, or who caused that to be?

Natural order and physical laws, such as gravity, establish the parameters for all other buckets of knowledge and learning. That is to say, all things shall proceed forth according to its order and abide by its laws, and we see this in our everyday lives. We get up, go to school or work, follow schedules and live in an orderly fashion. We generally tend to accept concepts like laws and order within our societies because they have always been part of our existence. They constitute a large portion of our conditioning and experience. The challenge: The routines of daily life condition us to believe we have "no control" over anything happening to us or around us.

I've discussed four buckets of laws important to the Mind-Morph Way and changing your life. Let's refresh:

Laws of Physics
phys·ics   / ' fiziks /   noun
The branch of science concerned with the nature and properties of matter and energy.

In school, we all learned about physical laws – laws that are typically indisputable and tangible. Examples of physical laws include time, space, sound, speed, and motion. You can probably think of several others. Laws of Physics are such a natural part of an order; their application is all-inclusive. People aren't born with an ability to defy gravity, for example. Scientific laws are indeed called "laws" because of the nature of physical laws (consistent in every manner). We can make extremely accurate determinations about much of the world around us based on scientific laws. This consistency is important for two reasons: First, because physical laws are such a part of our daily lives. If you think about it, even the air we breathe and every step we take is subject to and analyzed through the Laws of Physics (and science in general). Second, as you will read momentarily, the dreams, affirmations, visualizations, and desires you manifest in your mind can be created physically because of the fundamental consistency of physical laws. To create, we should understand our connection to the physical world, and how every thought and action we take affects this world.

Laws of Society

so·ci·e·ty / sə ' sīədē / noun
The community of people living in a particular country or region and having shared customs, laws, and organizations.

These are laws that we, like people, have designed and continue to sustain an effective existence in our society. We live within the constructs of these laws and agree to any consequence activated by breaking any specific law. The *consequence* is an important concept here. Generally speaking, consequence refers to the result of an action we consciously choose to take. For example, most societies believe stealing something that does not belong to you is bad for society as a whole. We can't have societies where people go around taking everyone else's stuff. So, there are laws in place which discourage stealing. Yet, some people still go around taking things that don't belong to them. They are subject to the consequences of breaking that law. Those consequences could be giving the stolen items back, paying restitution, or even going to jail.

As a side effect, societal laws – which have been around since almost the beginning of time – create a constraint: All things must either be *right* or **wrong**. The law says stealing is wrong. If you steal, then you are wrong. What if there is a situation where a man who has no money to support his family, steals a loaf of bread to feed his children? Is stealing in this scenario wrong? According to the exact letter of the law, yes. What about the spirit of what the law originally intended? On a deeper level, what would this say about a society that does not offer solutions for these situations? When a society allows its members to go hungry, then where does a violation of the law occur?

> CONSEQUENCE REFERS TO THE RESULT OF AN ACTION WE CONSCIOUSLY CHOOSE TO TAKE.

The challenge in this scenario is perhaps that society wasn't intending for someone who needs to feed his family to be considered unlawful. However, since the Laws of Society are definitive, people within societies accept the definition of laws and their consequences.

Concepts that define something as strictly right or wrong tend even further to constrain our thinking. Which then limits our ability to create our lives outside a predefined boundary set by others.

Laws of the Universe
u·ni·verse   / ' yōōnə vērs /   *noun*
All existing matter and space considered as a whole; the cosmos.

Mind-Morph combines an understanding of using universal laws, along with the other Buckets of Laws, in a harmonious manner. The Laws of the Universe is where the proverbial rubber meets the road.

While there are 12 Laws of the Universe, we will delve into

just a few of them here. There are two primary things to understand the Laws of the Universe. First, the Laws of the Universe encompass all things. By all things, I mean every-single-thing – trees, animals, people, technology, light, sound, and energy – everything. If a grocery cart rolls across the parking lot and bumps into your car, the entire string of events that caused that occurrence encompasses the Laws of the Universe.

Let's start with the universal Law of Attraction. The Law of Attraction says that like attracts like. Notice I didn't say positive attracts positive. Yes, that is true, and negative also attracts negative, which leads to the second item of understanding. Laws of the Universe act in a "push me, pull you" manner. For example, imagine two people facing each other, holding their hands in front of themselves, and interlocking fingers with one another. If both people push against each other, hand against hand, neither person will move. There is an equal force pushing in opposite directions. We used to play this game when I was a kid. It was usually fun if you were pushing against someone roughly the same size. As soon as the big kid came along, all he would do is knock the smaller kids over.

Imagine if both people, keeping their fingers interlocked, moved their arms fluidly together. Now you get a push-me, pull-you motion. If one person pushes one arm forward, the other person's arm moves backward. They are not resisting, just responding. Then, the backward arm pushes forward and that moves the forward arm back. The forward force causes a backward motion. See how that works?

Allow me to take this just a step or two further.

> LAWS OF THE UNIVERSE ACT IN A "PUSH ME, PULL YOU" MANNER.

Consider bouncing a ball against a wall. Maybe while practicing tennis, you hit a tennis ball against a wall so it would come back. You would adjust your position and your swing and hit it again. It would bounce against the wall and come back. If you hit the ball softly against the wall, it would come back softly. If you hit the ball hard, it comes back just as hard. That is how Laws of the Universe work. What you put out and how you put it out is what you get back and how you get it back.

Let's look at another example. The universal Law of Cause and Effect says everything you do causes other things to occur, and those things have an effect. Since the Universe brings back to you what you put out, those effects will come back. Again, the Universe does not distinguish between good or bad, positive or negative. It just returns the same energies that you send out, like hitting the tennis ball against the wall. Some may refer to this law as "you reap what you sow." If you put in good effort and do your best at something, you often reap good results. Doing a great job at work might result in a promotion or a raise. Likewise, if you go around gossiping or talking negatively to people around you at work, talk badly about your company, and generally have a poor attitude, then you may not get a raise or promotion or you could even lose your job.

As you grow from this point forward, remember, Universal Laws work in a get-what-you-give manner and apply to everything you do, say, and think.

Laws of the Spirit

spir·it　　　/ ' spirit /　　　noun
The nonphysical part of a person that is the seat of emotions and character; the soul.

Our individual spiritual beliefs or belief system principles are the basis for the Laws of the Spirit. Some examples of systems of beliefs are Christianity, Buddhism, Mysticism, Paganism, even Atheism. Your definition of "Higher Power" or "Infinite Intelligence" comprises your spiritual laws and beliefs.

Most spiritual belief systems can accommodate universal laws as part of the system. What is interesting is that spiritual law has been around much longer than our awareness of universal law, yet the two are intricately connected. Consider how science often proves the accuracy of biblical teachings. For example, the Bible uses the phrase "as the stars of heaven" to indicate a large quantity, i.e., Genesis 22:17 says, "...I will multiply thy seed as the stars of the heaven, and as the sand which is upon the seashore..." During biblical times it might have been easier to visualize what a large number the sands of the seashore represented. I don't know that people understood how many stars there realistically are. Today, with breakthroughs in technology like the Hubble Space Telescope and giant satellites, we've validated that the number of stars and galaxies and universes are innumerable – just like the sands of the seashore.

Recent discoveries such as these are important because they validate the foundation of the establishment of spiritual laws. Furthermore, these types of discoveries demonstrate the order and consistency of all things. For many of us, such discoveries also emphasize that God, or our Higher Power, is a part of all things. When we begin to discuss the process of *asking* in the next couple of chapters, consider what that means. What does it mean to you? Are we asking the Universe? Yes. Are we asking our Higher Power? Yes. For me, that means asking God. I do that through the power of prayer. Others may ask by spending time meditating or spending time in nature intentionally focused on needs or desires.

How and whom do you ask?

One More (Very Cool) Law Bucket – Quantum Law

Quantum Law or the Laws of Energy all refer to the study of Quantum Physics. A few years ago, I might have said the *theory* of Quantum Physics. However, we are WAY beyond theory now. Recently one scientist captured a picture of a single atom! At the most basic level, Quantum Physics shows us that everything, in its smallest measurable form, is made of energy. In humans, it looks like this:

People are blood, organs, muscle, skin, hair.
Cells form those physical traits.
Molecules form cells.
Atoms form molecules.
Subatomic particles form atoms.
Electrons bind subatomic particles.
Electrons vibrate rapidly, creating…energy!

John Assaraf is an entrepreneur who has built five multi-million dollar companies who also happens to be a leading behavioral and mindset expert. He says, "You and I are pure energy – light in its most beautiful and intelligent configuration. Energy that is constantly changing beneath the surface, and you control it all with your powerful mind."

Quantum Physics also says energy makes up all things at their subatomic levels. Energy is constantly moving – remember the push me, pull you effect of universal law? Every movement you make, every thought you have moves energy, and connects you with the Universe around you. And because you can move energy by thinking, YOU have the absolute power to CREATE. Let me say that again –

YOU have the power to CREATE!

Zzzzzzztttt! Record scratch! Whoa! Hang tight there, cowboy. Did I say that you have the power to create? Create what? How?

How about creating the path of your life, with your mind – your thoughts? Is that so hard to believe?

Why is it hard to believe?

Ok, I'll give you this one. It can be a bit of a challenge to accept this at first. Here's why:

It is difficult for our minds to perceive (see) something which we cannot first conceive (create or develop). One example most of us are familiar with is the invention of the airplane. I remember how weird it was to look in the sky toward the airport right after the 9/11 tragedy and not see a single plane flying around. They have become so commonplace it's obvious when they aren't there. In the late 1800s, even within scientific and engineering communities, many people believed it was a complete impossibility ever to get something heavier-than-air to fly. (As a side note, one thing I love about Orville and Wilbur Wright is they didn't have access to a lot of money, or any special knowledge or engineering. They did have one thing – a firm belief they could do it! And they did!)

Another example of something which was once inconceivable is the harnessing of nuclear power. In 1934, even Albert Einstein said, "There is not the slightest indication that nuclear energy will ever be obtainable." Today, we use it to power entire cities.

"I know this is a blind date, but I've decided to send some positive signals to the universe!"

Buckets of Laws

The tragic thing about all of this is that we, as societies, communities, religions, etc., have fostered the limiting beliefs of our people. Even today, we are uncertain of the method used to accomplish some things from hundreds of years ago. How was Stonehenge formed, how were the Great Pyramids made, how did the Aztec Indians have such advances in the making of tools, weapons, and medicines? During those periods, it seems thinking was allowed to flourish while creativity was promoted and encouraged – and amazing things were created as a result.

The Science

Some studies suggest our brains process roughly 11 million pieces of information per second, although we only consciously process about 40 pieces of information per second. One of the reasons for this discrepancy is that we are filtering everything. Think of it this way: The visual cortex – the part of the brain that processes sensory input from the eyes – is just like a camera lens. When a picture is taken with a camera, everything appears and is clearly visible. If a picture is taken of a child swinging on

> OUR BRAINS PROCESS ROUGHLY 11 MILLION PIECES OF INFORMATION PER SECOND.

a swing at the park, the picture would include the child, the swing and the swing set, the merry-go-round nearby, the see-saw, other children playing, every tree, grass, any birds flying around, etc.

If you were sitting on a park bench in that same scenario, and the child in the swing is your child, you would likely be filtering out everything your brain considers background noise to solely focus on your child and making sure she does not fall out of the swing. Because of that filtering process, even though our eyes see everything going on, our brain filters out the less important parts and focuses on the more important part. In this case, the focus is your child on the swing. As we move through the world each day and throughout our lives, our conditioning changes and evolves based on many experiences. Three have more of an influence on us than others:

1) Observation – we are constantly observing the world around us using every sensory input: hearing, smell, touch, images, sounds, etc.
2) Pairing – we automatically begin to match up events from all of this input to determine what is important. For example, we pair the heat with a hot stove to pain if we touch it.
3) Reward – we begin to determine what actions reward us and what actions do not reward us.

Take, for instance, a parent who does not value a clean home, who is not concerned about picking up dirty clothes, washing the dishes after a meal, or putting items away in a closet. Growing up with this parent, we would have watched their behavior and considered the cleanliness of the home unimportant; there would be no punishment for ignoring dirty clothes and dirty dishes. As such, we are much more likely to exhibit this same behavior later in life as part of our early conditioning.

Likewise, if our conditioning has been, and continues to be, that life happens to us, then our minds continue to find ways to reinforce that *reality*. And this is what many of us do day after day. We react to life around us and call it our reality.

Don't get me wrong; we have many forward thinkers and brilliant minds today. Bill Gates and the late Steve Jobs are two examples from the current "Connected Age." With all the billions of people in the world, why does it seem there are relatively few? Could it be due to the conditioning we go through? This conditioning has created limiting beliefs such as:

- Don't do that; it'll never work.
- You're not good enough.
- Everything is already done.
- What could you possibly contribute?
- Why would you ever want to do something like that?

See what I'm getting at? Can you see how the limitations we install by believing something is either strictly right or wrong? I think we have done a huge disservice to ourselves that way. How much more would we grow individually, and as a society, if we viewed things as either growing/evolving or not growing/not evolving? Perhaps we should be asking ourselves,

"Is this thing that I am doing moving me in a positive direction or a negative direction?"

"Am I growing myself by what I am doing or thinking?"

"Am I growing others by what I am doing or thinking?"

"Am I creating my reality?"

Connectedness

Most of us believe that each of the Buckets of Laws functions within its segment or silo. Believing that the influence of any category of law upon us is singular, not related to the others, maybe one of our most common limiting beliefs. All laws are connected, moving in and out and within each other constantly.

If you've ever seen or participated in a Soap Box Derby, then you know that the *soapbox* is a hand-crafted vehicle resembling a car and ***driven*** by kids with no fear. Soap Box Derby vehicles don't have an engine and rely on the Law of Gravity to pull them down a hill. The downhill race is the derby part of a Soap Box Derby. When someone says, "Ready, set, go!" they race to the bottom of the hill, relying only on gravity and the craftiness of their vehicle design to win them the race. The soapbox derby is an example of one of the Laws of Physics – gravity, operating by itself. The other law buckets are at work here, as well. However, you can see it *seems* as if there are no other influences.

If you were to attempt to do this same thing as an adult in a real car – that is, to start at the top of a hill and allow gravity to pull you down the hill – you would also be utilizing gravity and the Laws of Physics. If your vehicle was to gain too much speed,

causing you to exceed the posted speed limit and a police officer caught you speeding, then you would experience the mix of two categories of laws: The Law of Physics, where gravity pulled your vehicle down the hill causing you to speed and the Law of Society that says if you exceed the speed limit you are subject to a speeding ticket. The other law buckets are at work here as well, even though it *seems* like they are not.

Allow me to describe another example that will demonstrate a deeper mix of the law categories. Think, for example, of someone who has been on a long-distance drive all day and is drowsy. While driving, this person momentarily falls asleep, loses control of the car and crashes into another traveling vehicle. This

Law of Physics says that an object in motion remains in motion until acted upon by an unbalanced (or outside) force. In this case, that unbalanced force was another vehicle. As a result of the accident, the driver of the other vehicle dies. At this point, the drowsy driver is arrested, having violated the Laws of Society. Additionally, if the driver is of a Christian faith or other religion which values human life, he may believe that he has now violated a spiritual law or principle of his faith because he was directly responsible for killing another person.

In this scenario, we see a blending (an interweaving) of laws from three of the four categories – physical, societal, and spiritual. The other law bucket (Laws of the Universe) is at work here as well, even though it may seem it doesn't have an influence.

However, we know that energy is always moving, and all the events leading up to the car accident were set into motion by the thoughts, decisions, and actions of every person around that occurrence – whether they were directly associated with the accident or just an influence.

Author Andy Andrews, in his book *The Butterfly Effect: How Your Life Matters*, introduces a theory outlined in 1963 about how the flapping of a butterfly's wings sets in motion molecules of air that eventually could start a hurricane. Nearly 30 years later, science has proven this possibility. Even the force of a butterfly's wings can stir up the energy that contributes to the activation of larger wind gusts, which then contribute to the starting of a storm, which then contributes to the beginning of a hurricane. Andrews describes how the actions of people throughout history have had profound effects on billions of people even to this day: ***Every action has a reaction and an effect on the world.***

So, is it possible for you to create the path of your life instead of following a path you feel is placed in front of you? Yes, it is!

Purpose and Perfection

Understanding, now, all laws intertwine in all aspects, we further need to understand that all laws also work with complete purpose and perfection. To demonstrate this concept, and the ability for you to create your path, take a moment to rewind and think back through your life. Start the exercise with where you are in life today. Right now. Think of your job, your family, or relationship status, your finances. Spend a few moments taking a personal inventory of where you are right now. While you do so, think about how you are feeling about your current situation.

- Are you happy?
- Satisfied?
- Thriving?
- Anxious?
- Depressed?
- Uncertain?

Now, think back to the last big thing that happened that put you where you are. This catalyst might have been starting a new job, moving to a new place, getting married or divorced, having a child, or perhaps losing a child or another loved one. What was that event that put you in the world as you know it today?

When you have that fixed in your mind, go back a bit further to the event preceding that one – an event that led up to the catalyst.

- What was that?
- How were you feeling at that time?
- Was the world coming at you?
- Were you on a path, although not a path you created for yourself?

All of these events, despite the negative nature of some, occurred for a purpose and executed in perfection for the need at the time they occurred. That is the Law of the Spirit working for *us* and using the Laws of the Universe – which push us and pull us in various directions; the Law of Society – which affects us – interwoven with the Law of Physics.

All of those things affect all the people around us – friends, family, employees, and other business owners. And the ripples of all of that energy are still moving through the world today. We might even explain to someone, "It was so hard going through everything like that. Although, I would not be where I am today if it didn't happen the way it did." **Exactly!**

We are all connected to each other, and the universe by all of this and in all ways. And if you don't feel like you are in the best possible place you can be right now, then please understand this: ***There are purpose and perfection in all things.*** You are where you are right now because that is where you need to be. You are reading this book because this message is the message you need to hear right now.

- Maybe you were struggling spiritually and received this book from a friend at church.
- Perhaps your challenges are financial, and you passed by this book on your way to the Financial Planning section of the bookstore, not quite sure what made you stop and pick this book up.
- You might even be in such a place that *changing your life* is your only solution.

Somehow you've been sending a message to the Universe that you need *something* to help you. The Universe has led you here. And I can assure you – you have the power to create the world you want!

The real win happens when you consciously interrupt the dance between the Universe and your mind and intentionally design your world. This is *creating*.

If, after considering what got you to where you are now, you look forward to where you want to be, the logical question is, "What do I have to do to get there?"

Your Mind-Point

Take a moment to take stock of your Mind-Point as it relates to Buckets of Laws and your approach, beliefs, and understanding of these topics. Don't be surprised if you start seeing some of yourself in different shape categories. Buckets of Laws is an area where you could read all shape descriptions. Do you see any changes? Perhaps you believe a little more in the possibilities of all things? The possibilities for YOU. Change is Mind-Morph at work!

Typical **Triangles** will have a solid belief, understanding, and acceptance in laws that they can see, feel and experience. It may be more of a challenge to fully embrace abstract laws such as the Laws of the Spirit or Laws of the Universe. Keep exercising your willingness to believe outside your normal conditioning. Practice looking forward and answering the question, "What do I have to do now, to get to where I want to be?"

My **Diamond** friends may be getting a bit excited about the possibility of creating. I understand there may still be some hesitancy due to the uncertainty of where you want to be, or even the reality of what you need to do to get there. Hold fast and exercise faith in your Higher Power.

Many of you in the **Circle** category have likely embraced the concept of creating your path if you haven't already been doing it. Before you get too far, be sure to read the remainder of the book. If you start skipping fundamentals now, you may not have as much success.

Squares may feel a certain validation with the Buckets of Laws fundamental. What I mean by that is most Squares feel like they've always known there is a connectedness of all things, and just couldn't put the finger on it. Maybe you haven't thought of it in these terms before. Like Blues, you may want to run out and start creating this instant. Please continue to read first!

Your Buckets of Laws

Think about where you stand on various aspects of Buckets of Laws.

Which bucket of law do you see affecting you the most?

_____

_____

_____

Which bucket of law influences your life most often?

_____

_____

_____

How can you apply the Laws of the Universe to begin to improve just ONE aspect of your life?

_____

_____

_____

Write out what your most ideal life looks like to you.

_____

_____

_____

Write out what it would *feel* like if you were living your ideal life right now.

_____

_____

_____

_____

A True Story of Laws

Please allow me to continue my story of the young man I introduced earlier. As you might remember, he's attending to a Bible Church, and the Laws of the Spirit are swirling around him. He's 10 or 11 years old, so he isn't thinking of God all day, every day. However, he feels an influence on him he didn't feel before.

I wish I could tell you that everything in his life began to change for the better after accepting his newfound faith. I wish I could tell you that. I can't. In a fierce display of force, the Laws of the Universe kept bringing back to him what he was pushing into the world. He had no idea or concept of the Laws of the Universe, although they were hard at work doing what they always do.

Keep in mind; this young man is the oldest of three children living with a single parent. As much as he tried to keep everything that's happened within his family away from his mind, it still has a dramatic effect on him. He is doing poorly in school, he is not making friends easily, and he is embarrassed about hand-me-down clothes, worn-out shoes, and the free lunch ticket he has to get from the teacher before lining up to go to the cafeteria. His mind is a mess of negative thoughts and emotions. Those thoughts and emotions push him to negative actions, and all of this negative energy boomerangs back to him, day after miserable day.

One day on the mile-long walk home with his brother and sister an older neighbor kid pushed down the boy's brother. There was no provocation; the bully was doing what bullies do. Without thinking twice, the boy came to the aid of his brother and punched the bully square in the face as hard as he could. What happened next, he certainly hadn't thought about and hadn't expected. The bully hit the boy back just as hard!

Out of fear or shock (or maybe a little of both), the boy began to cry and ran the rest of the way home. When the boy's mom arrived home from work, the housing project courtyard was buzzing with what had occurred. When mom found out, despite the boy's plea not to do anything, she marched straight down the block to the nicely trimmed, two-story home with its manicured front and back lawns. She proceeded to give the father of the bully a piece of her mind – which she would find out later placed her right where he wanted her to go. He convinced her the two boys needed to have a boxing match to work out their differences. Why they could do it in his backyard, and he just so happened to have a couple of pairs of boxing gloves for just such an occasion.

Our boy, this young man whose own dad left him at the age of seven, who's been carrying the weight of caring for a younger brother and sister, who is struggling with grades, struggling with friends, struggling with everything is now being thrust into a backyard boxing match with the school bully twice his age. Could the world turn its back on him any further?

It doesn't take a genius to figure this out, and, let's face it, the boy's mom wasn't thinking this all the way through. It wasn't until they walked into the back yard she realized the bully is a Golden Gloves boxing champ. He's been boxing since he was five years old. He is warming up like he's in the Olympics.

The young man, with everything else on his shoulders, is beaten for the next nine grueling minutes, in three rounds of sparring for which he has not one minute of experience or coaching in his young life. He is now even more deeply embarrassed by all of the day's activities and does not incline ever to go back to school again.

He doesn't know it yet – this entire situation has set laws of the Universe in motion. The nature of those laws will affect him for the next several years of his life.

To be continued...

MIND-MORPH JOURNEY
BUCKETS OF LAWS

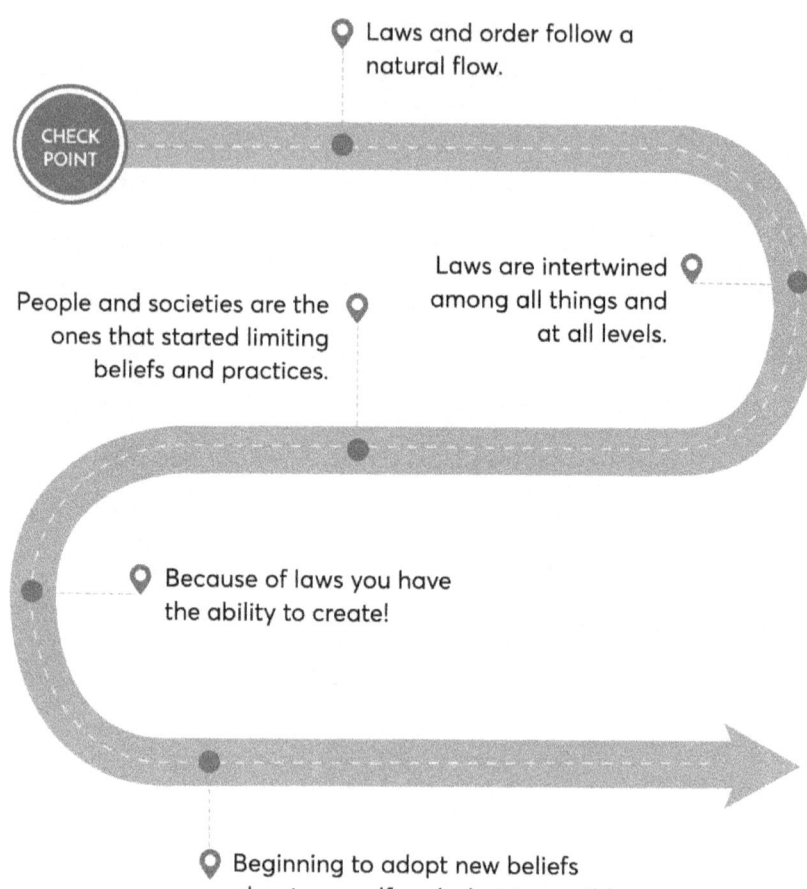

- Laws and order follow a natural flow.
- Laws are intertwined among all things and at all levels.
- People and societies are the ones that started limiting beliefs and practices.
- Because of laws you have the ability to create!
- Beginning to adopt new beliefs about yourself and what is possible.

Copyright © Chris Doyle, Mind-Morph

Chapter 4

#FlipTheSwitch

"Successful people imagine their ideal future, then work every day toward their vision."

Brian Tracy

Some days, just deciding what to have for dinner can be a challenge. And now, we're talking about making actual, life-changing decisions? *Real* decisions like where to live, which job to take, or with whom to have a relationship? You might be asking yourself, "How the heck am I supposed to do that?"

Well, I'm here to tell you! First of all, you're right. If you want to change your life, you must decide what you want. It is not just a "Yeah; I think I'll change my life" type of a decision, which sounds like a "Yeah, I think I'll take pepperoni pizza instead of sausage pizza" type of decision. We're talking about a *solid* decision here. A *Flip The Switch* decision, just like a light switch going from the *off* position to the **on** position. Yesterday, you weren't changing your life. *Today*, you are changing your life, and that starts in this chapter – *click!*

I've been asked, "If I'm already putting action around goals, doesn't that mean I've decided to change?" Not always.

Unfortunately, we can trick ourselves into thinking we've decided on something even if we haven't. Referring back to my smoking example in Chapter 1, and especially when it comes to addictions, we can put all sorts of actions into practice – we can visualize, we can attract, we can do a lot of things – and yet, some of us may ultimately slip right back to where we started. One reason for this is we started with the action while skipping the process of making the decision. OR, we decided for the wrong reasons – which is ultimately like not deciding at all.

You can *decide* you want to lose 20 pounds to be more attractive. If anything else enters into your mind that whispers, "You still aren't attractive," the first thing you are likely to do is to think to yourself, "Forget it! I don't need to lose weight anyway." Be assured, with Mind-Morph; you will overcome those thoughts.

I mentioned earlier, and as we have experiences and develop our conditioning, our brains are constantly looking for the reward or punishment surrounding our actions. It is also producing a specific chemical reaction for every one of those associations. Think about how you felt at a time in your life when you did something well. You might have been a great athlete, an excellent musician or artisan, or a high academic achiever. Perhaps you did something at work no one else could do. Maybe you were a superhero parent because you made the best peanut butter and jelly sandwich ever! Whatever your memory, think about how you felt at that moment. While remembering, you probably have a similar feeling now, and likely have a desire to experience that activity again. Here's what's happening: By recalling the instance, your brain produced the same chemical it produced during that event. It's the same process when we do well at work, when we do well at parenting, and when we do well at whatever we do. That chemical process is why gambling is such an addiction. When we win on a lottery ticket or at Bingo or Blackjack, our brains go into mega-production of that feel-good chemical (dopamine) and continues to do what is needed to have that same feeling again and again.

> YOU MUST FLIP YOUR INTERNAL SWITCH TO EXPERIENCE MIND CHANGE. #FLIPTHESWITCH

The same chemical process happens for anything we've ever felt rewarded for – even if the reward subconsciously came to us. Just as with positive, the chemical process occurs for negative activity as well. When we're angry, our minds are constantly getting us angry so it can reproduce the dopamine. Same thing with people who feed off drama, being the victim, or the attention they might get from being needy. Our brains continue to seek more of that feeling by repeating the behavior that preceded it.

The Science

Thankfully, we can override this system! You condition into behaviors, and you can certainly condition out of them – or into NEW behaviors. Until now, misbelief has been part of your conditioning. Now, you have to start new beliefs – visualizing and choosing your *new* conditioning. And as you are creating new beliefs and conditioning, you are *becoming* the person you most want to be.

"I stopped thinking of myself as just a clown, and now I own the circus!"

What is Conditioning?

We've talked a bit about conditioning and the characteristics we may have developed as a result of our experiences growing up. Conditioning is the habit of thought we develop as a result of our daily experiences.

Conditioning occurs as a result of two brain processes – deciding to take action (or formulating a belief), then creating a consistent habit of thought around that action or belief. These are two distinct processes, which occur in different parts of the brain.

The decision-making part of the behavior happens in a part of the brain, which is like a traffic cop. The habit-making part of the brain is like an interstate. Every thought we have and action we take reaches the traffic cop, so we can decide if we will do something. The traffic cop says, "stop." (The pause that occurs can be a long one, or so short we may not notice it. More on that later.) Then, after deciding, the traffic cop says, "go." Once we're given the "go" from the traffic cop, we proceed to get onto the interstate. If we've had this thought or taken this action before, then we cruise the interstate looking for memories, patterns, and emotions about that previous experience

Let's look at a practical example: putting on a seatbelt when you drive a car. First, you decide to put the seatbelt on, and in this example, you think, "Yes, I will put it on." Second, your brain looks for that previous experience, and that process looks like this:

1) An event occurs that tells the brain to go into automatic mode and let a behavior associated with the event unfold. For the seatbelt example, that could be getting in the car.

2) The routine kicks in and starts working. The routine is the part of the process we consider to be "habit." In the case of the seatbelt, the routine is that you reach over your left shoulder with your right hand, pull the seatbelt down and lock it into place.

3) And lastly, the brain responds to something it likes by creating a reward. It creates a positive association to help you remember the combination of this event and this routine in the future. In our example, the reward may be the pleasing thought that you will be safer with your seatbelt on if you are in an accident.

As this process continues to occur over and over, the decision part, where the traffic cop is, happens so fast we don't even realize we've already made a decision. We overlook our ability to choose when we're on "automatic pilot." Most of us would say we didn't even *think* about the process of putting the seatbelt on. It just happened. This is a brain mechanism that now takes these habits of thoughts and makes them so automated it doesn't have to think about them at all. That shortcut opens up more mental capacity to do other things.

How Were You Conditioned?

Now that you understand what conditioning is, you may be wondering how you've come into your conditioning, your behaviors, and your thought habits. Great question! I encourage you to think about what your answer to the question might be.

We are all so unique. Our experiences can never be the same. Even kids who've had all the same exposures and experiences growing up within the same family unit bring their perspectives, and therefore design their unique conditioning.

The process of creating habits of thought accounts for all our positive and negative actions. It also accounts for our great personal characteristics, and not-so-great character flaws. All of our brilliant, thinking-with-complete-original-imagination dreams and ideas, as well as all of our filtering, prejudices, and narrow-mindedness, are part of our conditioning.

Take a moment and think about some of the conditioning you've experienced in your life. Consider your upbringing, friends, and family. Think about various jobs, co-workers and bosses. Along with influences from your community.

Conditioning Can Be Changed!

To see how remarkable we are as people, you only need to see our abilities to change. Even people who have had strong experiences and deep-rooted conditioning can change their thoughts, habits, stereotypes, and prejudices. We do this because we have a wonderful gift called *choice*! We get to choose. Everything we do, say or think is a choice we control.

Since we get to choose what to do, say, or think, that means we can choose to change our current conditioning and establish *new* conditioning. In Mind-Morph, we call that *Flip The Switch*. Just like flipping a light switch on or off in a room at your house. This *flip* is the difference between what we believed before and what we choose to believe now.

> KARMA, MEMORY, AND DESIRE ARE JUST THE SOFTWARE OF THE SOUL. IT'S CONDITIONING THAT THE SOUL UNDERGOES IN ORDER TO CREATE EXPERIENCE.
>
> DEEPAK CHOPRA

It could be as simple as choosing to use a different color pen from now on. You might say, "I'm going to use pens with blue ink from now on instead of pens with black ink." If you have pens of both colors on your desk, instinctively, you may first reach for the pen with black ink. By "instinctively," we mean *without thinking about it*. As we now know, it isn't that we didn't think; rather, we thought so fast our actions occurred by habit – or habit of thought.

Changing our conditioning starts by first slowing down our

thinking until we recognize the habit, usually activated at the point of decision-making, and consciously made a different decision.

How to Change Your Conditioning

To break an old habit of thought and consciously make a different decision, you must catch the process as it reaches the traffic cop part of the brain. Decision making as it pertains to change is about overriding the habit. Remain aware and intentional about doing things in a new way.

What techniques work when you want to change a habit, and need to remind yourself to STOP - then take new action?

Create a Strategy

You know yourself better than anyone else knows you. Create a strategy that works for you. Here are some ways to change:

1. **Writing**

    Writing a note is one method that works well. In this example about changing pens, you might put a note in the same place as your pens so when you go to get a pen, you see the note first. This eye-catching note is a trigger to remind you of your newfound love of blue pens.

2. **Telling**

    You might say out loud each time you go to get a pen, "I

am using a blue pen!" Better yet, tell everyone you work with about your new habit. The more you say it, the more you believe it, and the more you live it.

3. **Remove Choices**

   You might even throw away any pen, which isn't blue. The equivalent of cleaning out the fridge for people who want to be intentional about losing weight. Or throwing away a pack of cigarettes for people who want to kick the smoking habit, which removes the trigger.

4. **Change Routine**

   Another method that works particularly well is to change any routine associated with the old habit. Such as moving your pens to the other side of the desk or into a different drawer. When you change the routine, it forces the brain to stop at the decision-making point and *think* before searching for memories about what to do next. And the brain will do this every time until this new action becomes a new habit. Breaking habits work well when you go away on vacation for this reason. All of your normal routines stop, and your brain is thinking about every small thing you are doing as it starts to create new associations and create new memory patterns. The brain is consciously processing decisions during vacation time, and people find it much easier to stop old habits and create new ones.

The Real "Why"

One of the challenges we face as we start to make different decisions to rewire our old conditioning is we sometimes choose to make changes in our lives for reasons which seem valid on the surface, but introspectively are not. I refer to these as "deceptive decisions." We sometimes *want* the decision we've made to work out, even though we have made those particular decisions on a shaky foundation. We think we know what we want, yet what we deeply desire is not immediately obvious.

Imagine a young woman who decided she wanted a dream home in an upscale neighborhood. She made her decision; she took action. She started by asking friends to help her make a list of all the items she would need to consider. Her list looked something like this:

1) Buy or build?
2) How many Square feet?
3) What kind of material – brick, stucco, etc.?
4) How large would the yard be?
5) How would she finance the purchase?

The list grew quite long. When the young woman realized there were several factors to consider, and began to feel defeated. After she met with a local mortgage company, she felt even more dejected when with the reality that she could not afford the home she had pictured in her mind.

After many questions about her dream home, the greatest came from her mentor: "Why do you want this dream home?"

Her first answer was honorable. "I would like to provide a wonderful home for my family," she replied.

"Why do you want to provide a wonderful home for them?"

"Because in such a wonderful home, my family will be comfortable and happy."

The mentor asked, "And why is that important to you?"

"If my family is happy, they will have a more fulfilled life."

"Will the home be the source of the fulfilled life?"

"Well, of course not," she answered. "Living a fulfilled life, an abundant life, will come from the love, and the teaching, and the patience, and the experiences my children will receive from my husband and me."

"I understand," replied the mentor. "So tell me, will the love, teaching, and patience be any different in a home which might not be as grand as the one you have imagined?"

In that instant, the young woman had what is known as an "ah-ha" moment. She realized she had created a story in her mind – centered around her conditioning – which fueled her belief that a large, expensive home was needed for her family to be happy and live a fulfilled life. That belief was not true at all. She could create the same loving environment anywhere! She realized, the outcome is the important thing

– not the house.

Another incredible thing occurred during this conversation and process. The young woman understood her initial reason for deciding to have a dream home in an upscale community was flawed. Her *why* – why she wanted the home – was based on a deception, a belief system she had been conditioned into throughout her life. Her family's happiness and abundance are her real *why,* and her motivation for success every day.

This experience, the ah-ha moment for this young woman forged her character moving forward in her life. She desired, more than anything, to become a woman who would give. She would give to her family, her friends, her community. At every opportunity she had, she would volunteer or take dinner to a needy family or lend a listening ear when someone needed comfort. She would *become* the essence of fulfillment for those she encountered.

Consider this: What is your greater WHY? Reach far beneath the surface level. Do not fall for deceptive decisions, counterfeits, or poor substitutes for what you earnestly want. Ask yourself two important questions with great honesty:

1. Why do I want this thing I have decided?
2. Who will I become as a result of this desire?

Your Mind-Point

Remember your Mind-Point. Which shape are you following for yourself? It is ok to read through all of the shapes to see if you are experiencing some change as you stretch your mind throughout the book.

Okay, **Triangles**, the act of making a decision may not be a challenge for you. However, embracing the concept that you can choose to change your beliefs or conditioning to make better decisions may be a challenge. My invitation to you is to try it with something small at first. Find a limiting belief you may have about something and consciously choose to believe differently about it. For example, you may have a coworker you feel can't do anything to your liking. Decide to believe that a person can do *everything* right for at least one week – and watch what happens. Additionally, think about WHY that decision would be important to you. Don't get trapped by the wrong why!

Diamonds, you may not have as much difficulty believing that you can make good decisions despite your conditioning, although you may fall prey to the pitfalls of not believing your decisions are *right*. Remember, Diamonds: There is not always the *right* decision. Sometimes, there is just a decision. I encourage you to choose a situation you might be struggling with and *go for it*! Check your why. If your why is solid, then see where your decisions take you!

Circles will want to believe all of their WHYs are true, and straight, and for the greater good. Circles can be a victim to deceptive decisions more than other shapes because they are traditionally more optimistic. My challenge to you is slow down on your next decision – no matter how minor it might seem – and dig into your why. Make certain your why contributes to the person you want to become.

Squares may have more of a tendency to feel like they have a solid WHY and take ownership of their decisions. For every decision you make, be intentional about what you are choosing. Strongly consider why you have made the decision, and if it will contribute to the person you want to become.

Flipping Your Switch

Take some time and think about *how* you have decided to make your life change. Do you own that decision? Have you decided for the right reason, the right WHY?

> What have you decided you want to add to, or change about, your life? Your decision can be one thing, or it can be many things. (However, if it is many, choose *one* to work on at a time.) Your decision is your Morph-Star!
>
> _____
> _____
> _____
>
> Write out WHY you want to change this thing. If the initial why is fairly surface level, give yourself permission to dig deeper and express the real why.
>
> _____
> _____
> _____
>
> What kind of person will this decision help you become?
>
> _____
> _____
> _____

Keep imagining the kind of person you can become. Would your future self do things that would contribute to a greater good? How?

_____

_____

_____

Describe what life looks like for you as a result of this decision.

_____

_____

_____

_____

A True Flip-The-Switch Story

While lying on his bed, after three rounds of boxing with the local bully, our young friend is not lonely, although he wants to be alone because he is feeling beaten. He is physically beat, as well as emotionally beaten and dejected. He is not fully aware of how to express his feelings or even how adults might explain them. They almost certainly included a raw dislike and mistrust for his mom. He doesn't realize she likely had good intentions, as misdirected as those intentions were.

In this moment of personal reflection, a flood of thoughts and emotions overwhelm him. As he cries in frustration, uncertainty, and self-pity, he makes a conscious decision which he will live by throughout his life. He decides that he would never be like his mother. He would be the opposite of what she represented at this moment.

- He would be a protector!
- He would be a provider.
- He would love more generously.
- He would understand more thoroughly.
- He would be a better teacher.
- He would be home for his children.
- He would cook for them.
- He would tell them bedtime stories.

- He would not let them become grown-up before they should!

Yes, this was a decision. A firm decision. And the reason? His WHY? Because he wants no other child in the world to have to endure what he has endured the past several years, which culminated in the conclusion of one fight, and the beginning of another – the fight for a good life.

To be continued…

MIND-MORPH JOURNEY
#FLIPTHESWITCH

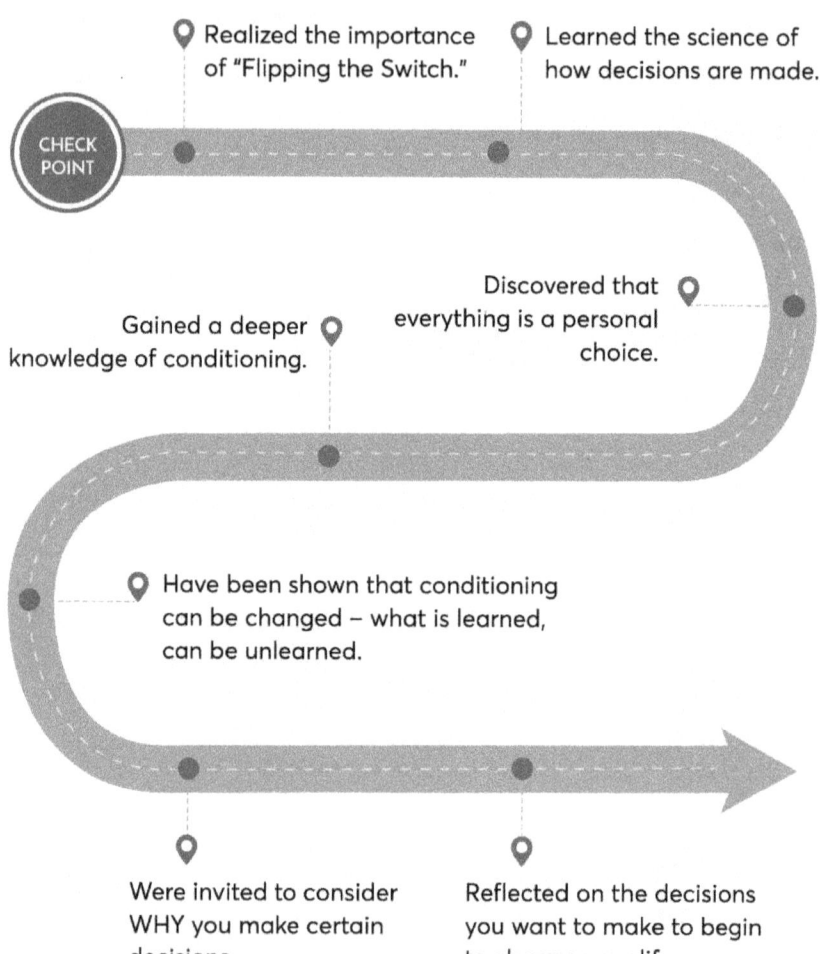

CHECK POINT

Realized the importance of "Flipping the Switch."

Learned the science of how decisions are made.

Discovered that everything is a personal choice.

Gained a deeper knowledge of conditioning.

Have been shown that conditioning can be changed – what is learned, can be unlearned.

Were invited to consider WHY you make certain decisions.

Reflected on the decisions you want to make to begin to change your life.

Chapter 5

Ready, Set, GET

"Ask, and it shall be given you; seek, and ye shall find; knock, and it shall be opened unto you."
Matthew 7:7

I'll never forget the time I was in my 8th-grade science class and the teacher asked if there were any questions from the group. One student in the back of the class raised his hand asking, "How do you grow raisins?" The entire room erupted in laughter. Some students rolled their eyes or mumbled. I remember someone saying something like, "Come on, be serious. Don't ask dumb questions." Even though the teacher thought the question was a funny one, thankfully, she explains raisins are dried-out grapes. She also explains prunes are dried-out plums. She continues to tell us about dehydration or something science-related. By that time I tuned out because I was feeling mortified for the kid who asked an innocent question. It's no wonder we carry fears surrounding *asking* through our entire lives. Talk about some negative conditioning!

The truth is, asking – for anything – is far more important and emotionally healthy for us then we understand. Think about how long you may have pushed a work project, waited before looking for someone to sew a costume for the school play, or wondered what to do about that knocking noise coming from under the car. Most of us believe we don't have trouble asking for help, even though we do.

What is Asking?

Within the philosophy of the Mind-Morph Way – changing your mind (changing the way you think) – asking is referring to asking for *something* and/or **asking** for help with something. We don't often have trouble asking curious questions such as, "How did you accomplish your success?" "Where do you want to meet for dinner?" or "What kind of music do you like?" Asking for something *from* someone is a completely different kind of "ask." For example, we often hear when we start a new job or take on new responsibilities at our company to "ask for help if you need it." Then, we will work late for several weeks as we "figure it out on our own."

One of the side-effects of our conditioning around this challenge is that it spreads over into other aspects of our life. Fear, uncertainty, and doubt surrounding asking other people translates to fear, uncertainty and doubt when asking in a more spiritual or universal setting, such as in the privacy of personal prayer or meditation. Asking God, the Universe, or a Higher Power seems as difficult as asking another person – if not more so for some.

Mind-Morph, and beginning the change in your life, requires the ability to ask freely. Ask for all things, from all those around you, from the Universe and God and the energy from the past, present and into the future.

"See? When you're not afraid to ask, great things can happen!"

Adopting a Growth Mindset

When you hesitate to ask, it is frequently associated with a fixed mindset around the object for which you are asking. When this occurs, I pose the question, *"What is stopping you?"* And, to answer the question I will have you consider which of three categories are most likely having a negative effect – 1) What is the real reason you are asking (*why*)? 2) Do you need to reset, reflect or realign your why/need/desire? 3) Is there a fear which may be overwhelming you? Within each of these questions, you will likely discover that you are thinking with a limited mindset instead of a growth mindset.

To embrace the admonition in Matthew 7:7 to "ask and it shall be given you," we must *believe* that asking creates the possibility to receive. Believing, and asking, can only occur if you think with a *growth mindset* instead of a fixed mindset.

Eduardo Briceno, Co-Founder and CEO of Mindset Works, an organization that helps schools and other organizations cultivate a growth mindset culture, delivers a TEDx talk titled *The Power of Belief – Mindset and Success*, where he quotes Stamford Professor, Dr. Carol Dweck. Dr. Dweck found that some people believe that ability and intelligence are *fixed* – meaning, what you have is all you have and you cannot obtain more. Other people believe that ability and intelligence are qualities that can constantly develop – a growth mindset.

At the beginning of the book, we discussed <u>The Mind-Morph Mechanism</u>. This mechanism is the process of orderly flow, which you follow as you implement life-change the Mind-Morph Way. We also explored <u>The ABCs of the Mind-Morph Mechanism</u>. The ABCs are the three easy checkpoints for making sure you can keep the system working for you.

If you are in <u>Section A</u> of the ABCs, then you are in the mechanism. You are likely in the forward-moving moment of any one of the five steps of achievement.

If you start to feel any slow-down in your progress, this is when I encourage you to move to <u>Section B</u> and ask yourself, "What is stopping me?" Take a look at the Common Achievement Annihilators later in the book and find your resolution path from <u>Section C</u> of the ABCs.

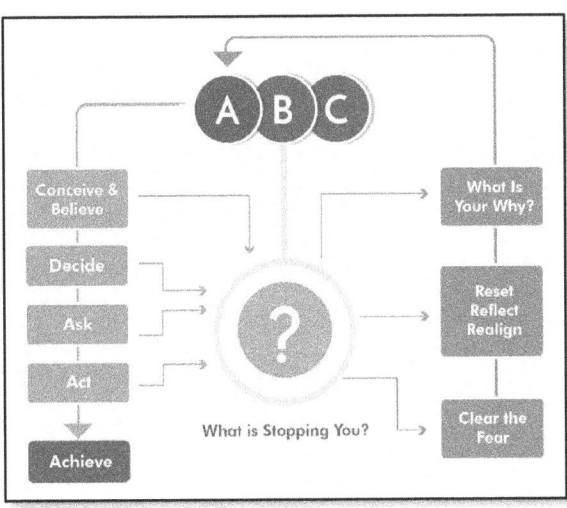

Following the Resolution Path

There are a lot of reasons we don't ask. These reasons are often personal, unique to our own experiences, well-known to us, or not known to us at all. I touch on some of the more common ones here. To the aspect of *asking*, I encourage you to consider what makes it difficult for you to ask for something. Asking yourself the question *"What is stopping me?"* is a good place to start. It will get your mind thinking around the various things that may be going on for you. Hey! I'll be the first to admit, there have been times when I could not put my finger on what was holding me back from something. To help here, let's look at the three most common categories that keep us from achieving our dreams and ideals.

What Is Your Why?

The first category on the Resolution Path is knowing *why*. I can't express enough the importance of understanding why you want or need something. Sometimes knowing *what* we are asking for can be fairly easy for us – I want a big house, a nice car, a great career, etc. It's the *why* behind the what that takes us off track. If your struggle is financial, it may seem as though if you had money everything would be fine. However, will the money help the root of the issue if what is most needed is help understanding financial planning or creating a budget? The same is true with most other needs. Why does it seem like when our car breaks down, the *only* solution is for us to get a new car somehow? When a *working* car is what we need. Especially if getting a new car will create a financial burden we aren't prepared to manage.

When practicing Mind-Morph, we are working towards creating abundance and living fulfilled lives. However, these concepts are rarely fully realized by obtaining material goods alone. When creating abundance, it is important to be clear on our personal *why*. *Why* are you asking for this "thing?" If your why is clear, then the *what* will naturally follow.

I can assure you of this – if the why is only for personal gain, it becomes almost an impossibility to obtain. Not saying it won't happen, however this type of why creates a misalignment with the universe around you, and that keeps you from abundance.

Reset, Reflect, Realign

The second category on the Resolution Path is to determine if you need to reset, reflect or realign. I devote an entire chapter to this concept, so allow me to describe what I mean here briefly.

When it seems like "something" isn't right, or the process doesn't seem to be working, it may be a matter of:

- Resetting – Change something you're doing or restart.
- Reflecting – Take time out to review your action plan.

- Realigning – Getting back in tune with your goals and desires.

Reset, reflect, and realign is where we need to turn when we are certain about our *why* and we don't have a particular fear holding us back.

Clear the Fear

Did you know, as humans, we are born with only two natural fears? They are the fear of falling and the fear of loud noises. That means every other fear we have is a learned, conditioned response. We might not know how we came to have a particular fear, although it is conditioning. As we now know, since we condition ourselves into it, we can condition ourselves out of it.

Understanding this now begs the question – *what is your fear?* I'm asking the question free of judgment. Be sure to ask the question of *yourself* free of judgment as well. Being judgment-free is important. We need to have honest awareness of the fears holding us back from the life we want to create. Do any of these apply to you?

- Fear of Not Knowing/Being Incompetent
- Fear of Appearing Weak
- Fear of Losing Your Job
- Fear of Incurring Indebtedness

- Fear of Asking for Too Much
- Fear of Rejection
- Fear of Succeeding

Which fears might you have which aren't listed here? While there are several tips and techniques available for overcoming fear, it often comes down to changing your thinking about the result. For example, if you are afraid of being rejected, then the mind-change is getting comfortable with, and taking ownership of, the only thing you can control in the situation – your response to the rejection. You can't control whether you do or you do not get rejected. You can control how you respond to the rejection. In a fixed mindset, someone might respond by thinking things like "I'm no good," "I can't do it," or "I know it's not going to happen for me." The Mind-Morph Way is to start thinking with a *growth* mindset. Growth mindset responses to rejection might be "I will continue to improve," "I know I can do this," and "I know it will happen for me at the right time."

The growth mindset principle is what Mind-Morph is all about. To change our *lives*, we must change our **minds**! We must have a clear comprehension of what we *honestly* want, **why** we want it, embrace a growth mindset and then –

WE MUST CLEAR THE FEAR!

Achievement Annihilators

Within each of these three categories – What is Your Why?, Reset, Reflect, Realign, and Clear the Fear – you will often find what I refer to as Achievement Annihilators. The mental blocks, or stoppers, which will keep you from achieving if you don't work on removing them. If you don't understand why, you will become bogged down in what feels like continual failure. If you do not reflect and realign your course from time-to-time, you could lose your focus or direction. If you don't overcome a fear, you will forever be stuck with a brilliant idea, and it will remain just that – an idea.

Several road blocks will keep us from the necessary step of asking for those things we genuinely desire. I've given you a list of some of the more common ones in the <u>Achievement Annihilators</u> section in the back of this book. Take a look and make sure one of them isn't keeping you from asking for the things that will help bring you into a life fulfilled.

The Science

Researchers have found that when people ask for help, our conditioning causes us to think in terms of how *big* the ask is. However, the people we ask, think first in terms of the *impact* of saying no to the person asking. For example, even though a potential giver doesn't immediately have access to money, they weigh their response in terms of "How will I feel if I don't help this person? What will it do to our relationship if I don't do this? And, am I taking on any trouble by lending assistance in this situation?" If the answer to a question puts the giver in a more comfortable position by helping, they would work to find money to lend instead of not helping at all.

Additionally, while we, as askers, become more fearful of asking the same person for help more than once, a study conducted on the campus of Stanford University shows positive results the second time a person asks. The study found the givers felt especially uncomfortable saying no a second time, so they were more willing to give. Perhaps this is an indicator of the value of maintaining persistence. Of course, I would also recommend gauging the response of the giver. If hesitancy or several conditions accompany the "yes" answer, it could be the giver is more likely meaning "no."

> CHECK OUT COMMON ACHIEVEMENT ANNIHILATORS IN THE SUPPLEMENT SECTION AT THE END OF THE BOOK.

Keep this in mind – developmental psychology research, by people such as Swiss psychologist Jean Piaget, indicates we have a natural response to make everything about "me." You may have needs. Your outlook may be bleak. Asking for help might be taking every ounce of energy you have. However, a "no" answer by the person you are asking may have nothing at all to do with you. Even those in positions to give freely can have circumstances within their own lives, which might prevent them from giving. We usually have no insight into their situation, and any rejection we receive still feels too personal. As if we did something incorrectly – we asked for too much, we asked too often, we didn't ask in the right way. When, in fact, we probably did all of those things perfectly. That doesn't change the giver's situation or their ability to give "at this time." It is so important to check your alignment, make sure you understand your why and stay open to the offerings of the Universe.

Are You Ready to Receive?

One often overlooked consideration when we are asking for something, is whether we are ready to receive it. What I mean is if you get the thing you desire so strongly, are you ready to receive it and to use it?

Here are some examples of not being ready:
If you are seeking a loan to start a small business and meet someone willing to finance the operation, and you don't have a business plan ready, you are likely to miss that opportunity.

If you ask to find your dream home and the one you have wanted for years goes on the market, and you don't have a down payment, you are not in a position to receive it.

If you have wanted a great job at a company and an offer comes to you, and you aren't willing to commute to their location, then you may have asked without being prepared to receive.

Review your circumstances. Consider what you are asking for and how the receipt of that thing will affect you, your family, your surroundings. Are you ready to welcome it today if you got it today?

A Formula for *Ask* Success

When it comes to asking, whether we are asking God, our Higher Power, Infinite Intelligence, the Universe, friends, family, or strangers, it can come with some fear, anxiety, and emotion. If you follow this little formula for success, you increase the likelihood that you are in alignment, and the process will net out in your favor.

1. **<u>Invite</u>** – When you ask the Mind-Morph Way, you first ask your spiritual power or search your intuition. This particular ask may include the questions "Is this the right

path? Am I asking the right person? Or am I ready at this time?" Asking is a form of prayer or search for spiritual guidance and direction. Approach this as an invitation to the presence of what you desire. Be clear, be humble, be ready to receive.

2. **Purpose** – Once you feel more positive spiritually speaking, connect all of your thoughts, energy, and actions into asking the Universe. You may not be sure who to ask. You are putting it "out there." Ask yourself, your spiritual power, and the Universe, if your desire is part of your purpose, if it contributes to a greater good, and if you are in a position to receive it at this time.

3. **Delivery** – Consider how you are asking. For those who are not good at asking or would usually not ask – START to ask. Again, humility and clarity work well. A softer approach can speak loudly to those ready to give. Remember, we are opening ourselves to the total possibility that the help we seek, the desire we want to fulfill, the abundance we are striving for is available in *any* fashion by *any* person or method.

4. **Give** – Be prepared to give. The *give* might be the repayment of a favor or loan. Or, it may be in a manner of paying it forward at a later time – helping another person in a similar situation to you or in need of your talents.

5. **Clarity** – Continue to ask at every point along your journey. Ask the next day for clarity or alignment again. Ask before each of your actions.
    - Is this right for me?
    - Am I taking on too much?
    - Am I asking the right people?
    - Why do I want it?
6. **Openness** – Be open to the answer and what the Universe is offering you. We sometimes think of openness as acceptance of the closing of one door and the opening of another. Sometimes there is no other door. You are where you need to be. Not seeing a door or opportunity might at first appear to be a *non*-answer. However, there are purpose and perfection in the answer.
7. **Create** – Remember, *asking* is the first of all ACTIONS. You are still actively creating and involved in the realization of your desires.
8. **Act** – Ask yourself to ACT! Don't stop after you ask.

As you get better at creating your path and become the person who believes in her potential, you will meet, attract and align yourself with people that *can* and **will** help you obtain all you need.

Your Mind-Point

Let's check your Mind-Point and see where you feel you are as it pertains to asking and receiving.

Consummate do-it-yourselfers, your preference is to not ask for anything, **Triangles**. You've likely had experiences where you were burned by not asking for help, and up-to-now you still haven't started to ask. There are two recommendations here: 1) Find a situation at work, home, church, you pick a place where you know darn-good-and-well you don't need a bit of help and get someone to help you with *something*. Make it up. Have the person that sits by themselves at church hand out the program, ask an assistant on the baseball team you coach to lead a practice, delegate a report to a subordinate at work. Just get in the practice of asking. 2) Start asking your spiritual power and/or the universe for some of your lower-profile needs. Beginning to ask might be helping you overcome a grudge or touching the heart of someone holding a grudge against you. It could be coordinating things perfectly, so you get the best seats for your family at the ball game. As you learn to communicate more easily in all aspects, you will start to see more things unfold before you.

Not necessarily the complete do-it-yourselfer, there is still an element of not asking that comes with being a **Diamond**. Diamonds are *usually* (not always) the ones that put off, and put off until it is so late you no longer have a need, rather a full-on crisis. Understandably, there is fear and conditioning at the root of this behavior. Start by asking yourself if living in this way is a help or hindrance to most aspects of life. Then, the most practical thing you can do is intentionally work to get a hold on *at least ONE area* of your life where you need help. That may be asking someone to help you go through the pile of bills on the table and paying everything overdue. It may mean reaching out to a colleague to help organize your workflow. It may mean asking a friend to help clean your garage. Spiritually and universally speaking, ask for open hearts of the people you reach out to for help AND ask for energy to begin to be more proactive and taking assistance where you need it.

Circles, you may already be comfortable with asking. I encourage you to continue to practice and refine your asking – be more clear, be more open to receiving. I will also remind you not to be the over-asker. Don't be the one who is constantly asking for everything and cannot seem to do anything without someone else's help. That is also not positive growth or creating your path. You may consider changing your "ask" to "How may I help you? Is there anything I can do for you today? Or, what can I do to get better results?" I invite you to check your spiritual position and make certain you are giving as well as receiving.

Squares, you too may be quite comfortable with the art of the ask. If you aren't practicing regularly, take an opportunity to write some areas where you can build a network of resources that will help on your current journey. Part of asking might be asking people to mentor you to help further your growth and development. Prayerfully or spiritually, consider and ask where you are needed to give of yourself. Remember giving of your time is as valuable as giving money.

Ready, Set, GET

Start by identifying reasons you aren't asking. Choose which characteristics are obvious and then think through some of the ones you might possess which are less clear to you.

_____
_____
_____
_____

List out some of the fears you have, which are keeping you from asking for your biggest goals or desires.

_____
_____
_____
_____

From your list of fears, write out ONE, which you consider your biggest concerning your Morph-Star.

_____
_____
_____
_____

For your ONE biggest fear, what are three things you can do to begin to overcome that fear?

_____

_____

_____

_____

Of the things you can do to begin to overcome your biggest fear, identify ways you could ask for help removing the fear. Remember, no 'ask' is off-limits. Think as widely as you are able.

_____

_____

_____

_____

In Chapter 4, you wrote down at least one thing you want to add to, or change about, your life. Now write WHY you want to make that change.

_____

_____

_____

_____

Describe how and who you will ask as you start to fulfill these desires and create your abundant life.

_____
_____
_____
_____

Describe the ways you are ready to receive the things for which you are asking.

_____
_____
_____
_____

A True Story About Asking

As you may remember, the young man whose story I have been sharing with you had made a firm decision at the end of a difficult day that he would not live his life the way his mom had been living hers. He did not realize at the time he was having a grown-up conversation with himself in his mind. He proclaimed to God and the Universe that he wanted more than what he'd been getting up to that point. His decision was final, and his reasoning was profound and meaningful. Of course, he had no idea what it meant to create a better life, except, of course, it would just be *better*.

As his emotions wound down and the sunlight began to fade to darkness, he started something he learned at church this past year and which would become a comforting practice throughout his life. He prayed. He asked God to make things better. To take care of him, his brother, his sister, and his mom. Help them find a nicer place to live. Help his mom find a job that paid more money. Help them get a car that runs better than what they have now. There seemed to be too many things they needed. How would they get them? Where would they find the home, the car, or the job? "I don't know how to get them," he said out loud, "please…"

Perhaps it was the intense energy or emotion this boy embodied in his pleas for help. Maybe it was the combined energy of a struggling family, all asking for the same thing in the solitude of each of their hearts. God, and the Universe, began to deliver with a tremendous force. While not his expectation (although he wasn't quite sure what to expect), over the next several months, each thing he asked for is realized.

His mom met a man and began a lengthy relationship. While the new boyfriend's primary career wasn't auto mechanics, he knew quite a bit about cars and helped the family find an adequate upgrade. The man also contributed a bit financially, which facilitated a move out of the housing projects and into a nicer Section 8 single-family home. The new home was, by far, better than anywhere they have lived up to now. Since mom had more reliable transportation and some help watching the three kids after school on occasion, it allowed her to find a better paying job – which she did!

Not everything was completely smooth sailing. After all, there is another new school to figure out and new friends to find. There is still little money – the family went from extremely poor to just poor. And there is still taking care of a brother and sister without a dad. Even at the tender age of 11, this young man knew enough to be grateful, thankful and indebted to whatever, and whomever brought about the much-needed answers to the prayers for a more abundant life – and he was learning the benefit of asking.

To be continued…

◉ MIND-MORPH JOURNEY
READY, SET, GET

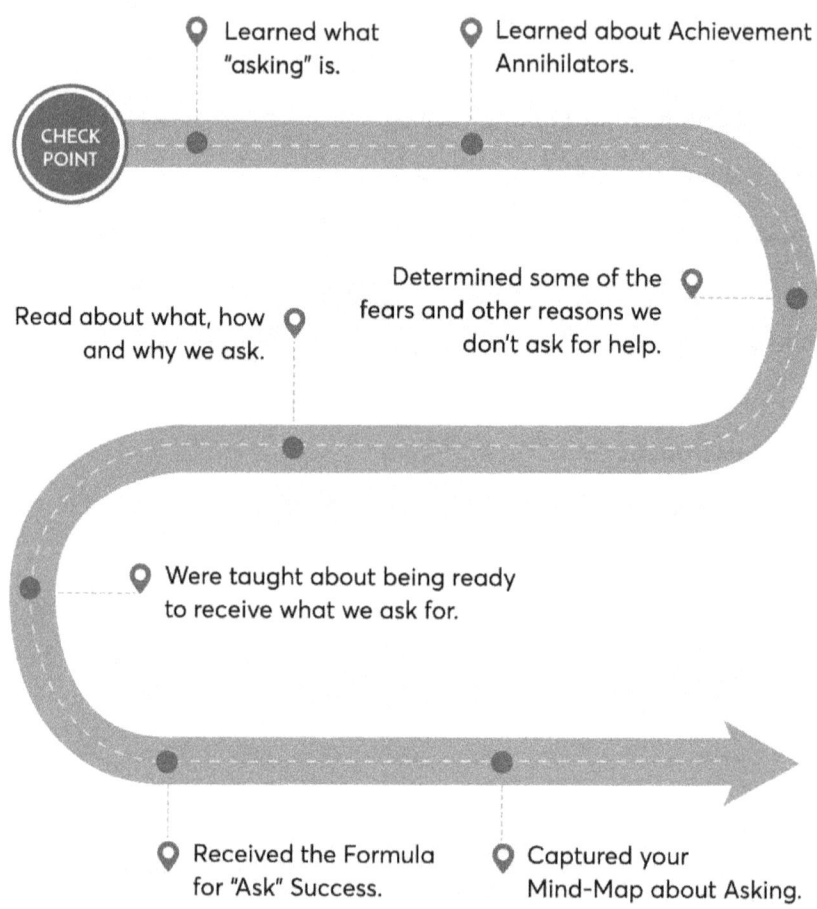

- Learned what "asking" is.
- Learned about Achievement Annihilators.
- Read about what, how and why we ask.
- Determined some of the fears and other reasons we don't ask for help.
- Were taught about being ready to receive what we ask for.
- Received the Formula for "Ask" Success.
- Captured your Mind-Map about Asking.

CHECK POINT

Copyright © Chris Doyle, Mind-Morph

Chapter 6
"Action" Isn't a Noun

"Action is what turns human dreams into significance."
John C. Maxwell

As we've been on this mind-changing journey together, I've explained how you can begin living the Mind-Morph Way and how the Mind-Morph Mechanism works. So far, you've heard about *believing* in your idea (your Morph-Star), making the firm *decision* to pursue it and **asking** God or your Higher Power, the Universe, and those around you while you seek to achieve your desire. Now we're at the point where the realization of your dreams starts moving – putting your thoughts and ideas into *action*.

As you continue to live the Mind-Morph Way, remember to keep thinking, and acting, with a growth mindset, as though all things are possible. You may not know how it will come together. However, your Morph-Star *will* come together for you. As you have been following the chapters of the book and completing the question segments, you have already started to practice. Your engagement with the book, in and of itself, is taking action. Take a fresh look at your previous answers and rewrite them below.

From **Chapter 2** – Write out the beliefs you currently have which you feel *will contribute to* the achievement of your Morph-Star:

_____
_____

From **Chapter 3** – Write out what your most ideal life looks like to you.

_____
_____

From **Chapter 4** – What have you decided you want to add to, or change about, your life? The decision can be one thing, or it can be many things. (However, choose ONE to work on at a time.) This is your Morph-Star!

_____
_____

From **Chapter 5** – In Chapter 4, you wrote down at least one thing you want to add to, or change about, your life. Now write out WHY you want to make that change.

_____
_____

What has changed in your thinking about your Morph-Star up to now?

_____

_____

The processes of thinking through these questions, and physically writing your answers is positive action. You are already engaged in creating your ideal life. Keep going!

Working Backward

It may seem logical to take a linear, step-by-step approach to reach your ultimate goal or achievement. And that is true to an extent. After all, you can't build a lemonade stand and go straight to depositing your quarters at the bank. There's the need to buy lemons, mix the perfect recipe (the right balance of sweetness to tartness), determine market price, and maybe even do some roadside marketing.

However, sometimes, the *next* step isn't necessarily a clear one. When this is the case, one good technique is to start with the end in mind and work backward to where you are now, keeping track of all of the little steps along the way. It's easier to see how this works if you start with something you already know. For example, pick a place in life you are now. Are you married or divorced, with children or without children, working or not working? Choose one area and think back step-by-step about how you arrived right where you are today.

You don't have to go too far back to get the idea of how this works. Do you see how each progression leads to another opportunity? I like how this process also demonstrates the *purpose and perfection of all things*. While some of your choices and actions seem bad on the surface – and might have been hard to go through – they ultimately led you to exactly where you need to be.

To apply the same concept to something that has not yet occurred, start with what you feel the perfect end-result would be. If we take the lemonade stand idea, those steps going backward might look something like this:

- ▶ I want to have a profit of $100,000.
- ▶ I need to open a bank account to deposit the profits.
- ▶ To open the bank account, I need a business license from the city office.
- ▶ Before I get my business license, I want to make sure I can make money in the lemonade stand business, so I research competitive lemonade stands.
- ▶ Develop a lemonade recipe better than any I've tasted.
- ▶ Create a better concept for the stand, i.e., bistro tables under a shade tree.

Again, this is just an example. Can you see how I am moving backward in the progression, and as I do, I am hitting on some action items I need to get moving on? In this case, it almost doesn't matter where I start, as all of the items have about the same importance, and all of them need to get completed.

If the process starts to seem overwhelming as if there is *too much* action to take on, determine the smallest, easiest thing you could do first and start with that.

Brainstorming

Another good technique for determining your action items is brainstorming. Brainstorming is great using the right philosophy – that *all* ideas are good during the brainstorming session. Of course, you are going to get some silly, make-no-sense concepts, and that's the fun of it! And, you never know which of the no-sense ideas are the homerun you need.

To start brainstorming, you need one idea you want to explore further. I suggest doing it either with someone who will take notes or recording yourself. Sometimes you can get going with many ideas at a fast pace, and you may lose some as you try to capture them on paper. I recommend inviting as many trusted, supportive people for your Circle as you can. There is truth to the phrase, "Two heads are better than one!"

Again, when you start brainstorming, the only rule is there is no such thing as a bad idea. You are trying to capture anything and everything you can. You probably know almost everything about your original idea already; chances are you have been thinking about it for days, months or even years! Here are some questions for you to consider to try and get out everything rolling around in your "noggin" and to put some action around that thing you most want:

- *Why* do you want to do it?
- How does it look in the end?
- Who do you have to become for it to succeed?
- What do you need to buy?
- With who do you need to connect?
- What do you need to learn?
- Can you describe your perfect customer?
- What are you willing (and not willing) to sacrifice while you are making it happen?
- What equipment, space, or other physical resources do you need?
- Can you start with items that aren't brand new?
- What do you need to avoid to be successful?
- Who or what will help you be most successful?

Remember, even after a good brainstorming session, your list will not likely contain everything. It's ok to keep adding, removing, or changing items on the list. Refining is a natural brain change process.

Once you have a list, complete or not, go through and prioritize the *top three* actions. You will be able to recognize them. For example, if you are starting a business and it requires a physical building or highly visible location, finding that space would likely be in the list of top three priorities.

When you have your top three actions chosen, for each one of those three, write down the steps you need to take to start and/or complete each item. If some steps seem big or overwhelming, break them into smaller steps. You will now have your next several action items in place.

Affirmations

Like brainstorming, the mental process of developing affirmations will stimulate your creativity, refine, and solidify what you want to achieve within your Morph-Star. Affirmations are a declaration of the accomplishment of your desires. It is a written statement further supported by positive thought and attraction. In Mind-Morph, I refer to positive, forward-looking, growth mindset statements that help us stay focused and aligned with reaching our abundant lives. For example, if I am in the process of looking for a better job, my affirmation might look something like this:

> *I have a job I love, which fulfills my mental, emotional and financial needs with a company that values their employees.*

Unlike brainstorming, which is more effective with more than one person, affirmations tend to be more personal. Furthermore, as you become better acquainted with the benefits of affirmations, you may want to create one for each aspect of life you most want to grow. It is not uncommon for someone to have a *life* affirmation or vision, a *financial* affirmation, and a *career* affirmation.

> WHO DO YOU NEED TO BECOME TO ACHIEVE YOUR IDEAL LIFE?

I invite you to think of your affirmations without regard to your age, current financial situation, etc. What does your ideal life look like to you? Also, always state your affirmation in current terms. For example, "I am." Not "I want," "I will be," etc.

My life-affirmation looks like this –

I am a financially independent servant leader committed to building the Kingdom of God on earth. I do not tire in my efforts to lead, teach, coach, and mentor in any capacity. I function in work- or service-based capacity for 9 months and dedicate my time to my family and friends 3 months of each life year. I live enriched, fulfilled and at peace watching the sunset over the ocean.

Do you see how that touches on the aspects of life that are important to me? It's a life-affirmation, so I am not specific in each item. I'm also not specific because I am open to however God (and His universe) may deliver it to me. For example, in my ideal life, I say I am financially independent. Others, who prefer to be more specific, may say, "I have 10 million dollars in the bank."

If you choose to be more specific for your other ideal life areas, for example, your finance affirmation may look something like this –

I earn one million dollars before the end of my 50th life year.

I've earned ten million dollars by the age of 55.

Notice, I won't say how it will happen here. You might establish that in your life-affirmation.

A work/career affirmation might say this –

While maintaining a quality work/life balance, I extend every possible effort in my business endeavors to uplift and edify leaders by sharing my gifts of knowledge and skill through personal development, coaching, leading, and mentoring. I accomplish this daily by exemplifying my faith, continually studying and refining my craft, exercising good and honest business practices, and accepting the opportunities the Universe presents to me.

See how that works? You would do that with any of the ideal life areas you are working to change, or improve. Don't overwhelm yourself. If you create goals and affirmations in every area, it can sometimes be hard to try and master them all. You will be amazed at how concentrating in one area can even help improve other areas.

You can certainly type affirmations out on the computer until you get the wording the way you want, however it is best to write them out physically.

To get the most from your affirmations, you will also want to say them out loud. Repeat them each day (and more often if you like). Keep them in a place that is visible to you regularly. When affirming your desire and intention, *FEEL* the result. It must be an integral part of *you*. Who you are. Who you are to become.

"Now all I need to do is brainstorm the steps between numbers two and three!"

The Science

Now that you have some great *take action* ideas let's dive into the science around some of what I am having you do – not just in this chapter, as an overall principle throughout the book.

I was curious about the process of physically writing as a method of finding greater success. I found an article published in Scientific American, which discusses the trend of college students using laptop computers to take notes during class instead of writing notes on paper. Simple observation shows students taking notes with the computer capture much more of what is said by the professor. Because students can type faster than they can write, and depending on how fast a student can type, they may be typing nearly all of what a professor says.

The research was conducted to see if there was any evidence to support better performance by students taking typed notes versus students hand-writing their notes. The results showed students who wrote their notes by hand outperformed the others in their overall understanding of the material and their ability to apply and integrate the material.

The reason for this is writing is a slower process that forces the brain to digest, summarize and capture the essence of the writing. In short, the brain *processes* what we are writing, while we are writing. And because it does that, we have greater comprehension and retention when we write things out. In the Mind-Morph Way, we might say when we write out our dreams, goals, tasks, etc., we are taking full ownership of them within our single biggest resource – *the mind*.

Time to Get Started

Now it's time to get started with putting action into your, well, *actions*! There is truth to the expression: *There's no time like the present.* Mostly because all the distractions that will keep you from starting now will still be there in the future, so start now while you are determined.

You know yourself better than anyone, so you will find the personal rhythm that works best for you to begin and keep going.

Some reminders:

- You've been in action since you started reading this book. Keep that momentum!
- Start with the smallest, easiest action. That success will lead to the next action and then to the next.
- Write, recite, and live your affirmation(s).
- Keep asking – ask for direction, ideas, support, anything you need to reach your Morph-Star.

If you get stuck in your action items, go back to the ABCs and ask yourself, "What's stopping me?" It's those Achievement Annihilators that will creep in and keep you from fully completing what you want to achieve.

If you need some direction on where to start figuring out your action items – or if you feel like you need to realign or reset – use the Take Action Survey I've included at the end of the book. It is a great way to think about what you need and where to start. (We'll take a closer look at how to reset, reflect and realign in the next chapter.)

Tips to Speed Up Results

In addition to writing out your goals, desires, and task lists, you can also use these methods to speed up the rate at which you begin to see positive results.

We've discussed brainstorming and affirmations already. Some others are:

- **Visualizing** – See your Morph-Star happen in your mind daily and even multiple times a day. Remember, if the mind can conceive and believe, it can achieve.
- **Mentors** – I've made this statement before, and it is worth repeating. Connect with individuals you admire who you feel have achieved at the level you want to reach. Ask them if they will mentor you through your journey. Most consider it an honor.
- **Verbalizing** – Tell trusted people* about your plans. Even if it takes years to fulfill your Morph-Star (it certainly did for me), others will continue to support your efforts.
- **Help Others** – If you find yourself struggling to learn a topic, teach it to someone else. You will be amazed at how much you learn by sharing and teaching someone else. The same is true for Mind-Morph. Help others reach their Morph-Stars, and you will reach yours.

A note here – Some people in our lives may want us to remain where we are, so be reminded of this when choosing who to talk with about your Morph-Star.

Your Mind-Point

Here's one action item you can perform this minute – check your Mind-Point! Many things can get in our way and keep us from starting and maintaining the act of *doing*. I'm going to show you where each level may tend to lean. Keep in mind that we are all human, and *life* shows up for all of us.

The key to taking action is to override whatever it is that keeps you from doing it.

You will be more likely to take particular actions, such as starting a new business, or committing to a long-term relationship, if you have witnessed someone else doing it successfully. My encouragement to you is to step beyond your comfort zone. Other people's experiences can be a positive example of what your personal experience can be. Take a chance; take the plunge. Prioritize your task list and perform Item #1 today. If you are doing it the Mind-Morph Way, you will be at peace no matter your level of success, *and* you will be glad for your experience.

You often mimic your friends and colleagues. Following can serve you well and sometimes it may not serve you well (I won't bring up that time in high school). While you may be good at playing follow-the-leader, the *leader* may not be going in the best direction for you. Remember, when you are living the Mind-Morph Way, there is no such thing as failure, only learning opportunities. What action will you take first, knowing you can't fail? Have a brainstorming session to capture your action list – do that now!

You may already be engaged in some action items toward your ideal life, and that is fantastic! I'll remind you not to stop now. Keep it going! If you feel like you are slowing down or you get stuck, go back to the ABCs and determine if you need to rethink your *why*, reset, reflect, realign or clear the fear. If you do that, you are certain to reach all you desire. Pause here for a moment and write an affirmation surrounding the achievement of your Morph-Star. What does reaching your achievement look like for you? What does that feel like for you?

My bet is you are well into listing your action items and may already have started on your easiest task. Keep checking the *why*, reading, and reciting your affirmation(s) and staying in alignment. Check the ABCs if you feel a slow down or to reignite the spark or passion you have for a life fulfilled. Take a moment now and cross off any items you've accomplished on your task list, determine what's next and schedule your time for that task.

Action List

The only item to capture in this chapter is to list the 3 FIRST actions you need to perform to achieve your Morph-Star.

_____

_____

_____

_____

_____

_____

_____

A True Story About Taking Action

I've been sharing this story about a young man I know. Up to now, I've explained some meaningful events that shaped his character and the course of his life in his youth. Allow me to move ahead a few years into his teens. Up until about the 8th grade, he hadn't been a good student. When you are more concerned if (and what) you are going to eat for your next meal, who can concentrate on items as trivial as school?

Now, in the 8th grade, he'd been exposed to much more of the world than what he had known living in the somewhat secluded life of public housing. He is seeing, for the first time, the joy people could have by having money. He is experiencing his first glimpse of the *possibilities* of something he'd known quite little about until now: **potential.** He enjoyed something that he would cherish and value the rest of his life – the encouragement of a caring teacher.

At this perfect moment, when he needed it most, he was awakened to a concept he hadn't considered before. He began to understand people could become more than they are, there is a way to make a better life, and you do not have to be resigned to live as you have in the past. What a concept! What a joy! What a blessing this is to people such as this young man!

He determined, over his 8th-grade year, that his life would be better than it had been until now. He resolved in his mind and his heart that he would rise above his current social status, financial status and abilities. And he did just *that*!

He started to work toward better grades and develop closer relationships with other kids, teachers, and people within the community whenever he could. He got involved in sports and clubs, including the Fellowship of Christian Athletes. He took the action he needed to reach the levels he wanted. He didn't want to be a good student; he wanted to be the *best* student. He didn't want to know some other kids; he wanted to know *all* of the kids. He didn't just want to achieve; he wanted to *overachieve*.

He didn't know what he was doing at the time, although he was living the Mind-Morph Way. He'd decided what he wanted, he knew why he wanted it, he was asking for direction, guidance and help when he needed it and he was listening to people he trusted and taking action so other people around him would forget about…

- *his poverty level*
- *his social status*
- *his previous bad grades*
- *his previous destiny*

And . It . Worked .

To be continued…

📍 MIND-MORPH JOURNEY
"ACTION" ISN'T A NOUN

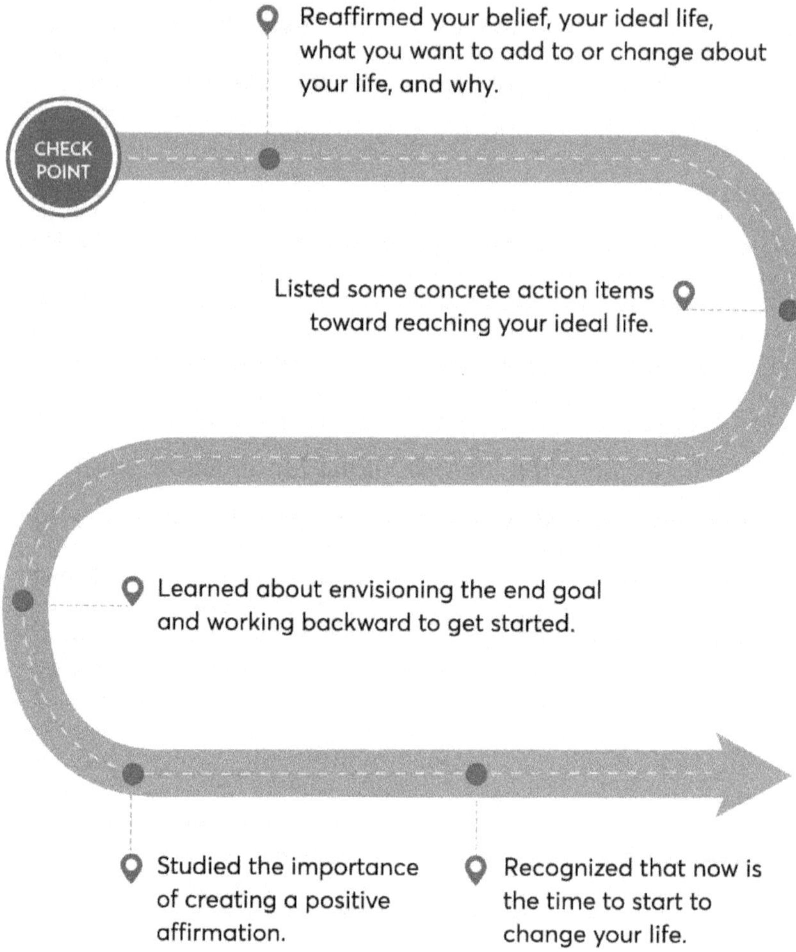

CHECK POINT — Reaffirmed your belief, your ideal life, what you want to add to or change about your life, and why.

Listed some concrete action items toward reaching your ideal life.

Learned about envisioning the end goal and working backward to get started.

Studied the importance of creating a positive affirmation.

Recognized that now is the time to start to change your life.

Copyright © Chris Doyle, Mind-Morph

Chapter 7

Reset, Reflect, Realign

"I can do all things through him who strengthens me."
Philippians 4:13

As a "computer guy" at the onset of the personal computer era in the mid-1980s, I recall how often I told people to *reboot* their computers. It was pretty much the go-to solution when nothing else seemed to fix a problem. Since then, the term *reboot* has taken on a life of its own, used in many different contexts.

"We need to reboot this project."

"I'm rebooting my workout effort."

"We decided to reboot our relationship."

Overall, the meaning is the same – shut down what is currently happening and restart it as new. The concept also applies to life-changes and mind-changes. Sometimes we get so caught up in what we are doing, then realize we've drifted way off our original course and need to get back on track.

If you find yourself in <u>Section B</u> of the ABCs – that spot where something is keeping you from moving forward, take a timeout and see what might be stopping you from reaching your desired achievements. You may need to take time to *reset, reflect,* or *realign*, especially if you are pretty solid on *why* you're striving for your change, and you sincerely believe you aren't fearful of anything.

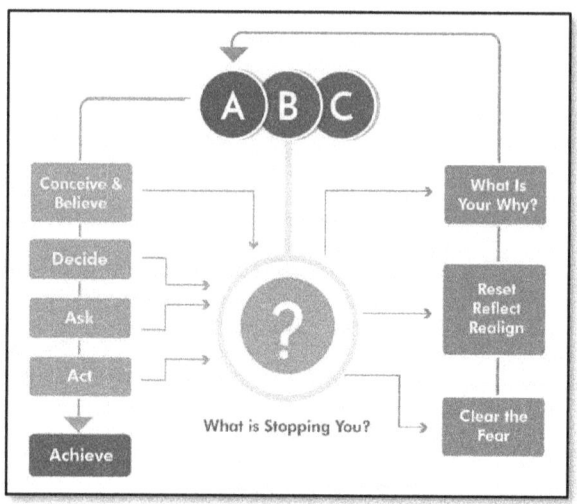

Reset

While each of these – reset; reflect; realign – are all similar to some form of rebooting, *reset* is probably the closest action to pressing <CTRL> + <ALT> + <DEL> on your human keyboard.

I can think of several times I ran down a path, certain it was where I should be going. Disappointment ensued, and I missed my expectations. If I had stopped long enough to adjust, I probably would have ended up closer to my initial goal.

I now consider times like those as learning moments. I had reasons for doing what I did, however they were shallow, or I had not "thought them out." I was actively engaged, however my actions were haphazard and often meaningless. More importantly, I didn't stop to ask if *this thing* I was doing was what I should be doing. I wasn't asking if there was going to be a benefit to anyone (besides myself) – if there would be a positive impact on my family, friends or the world around me.

If I had the opportunity to live out any of these "learning moments" again, using hindsight, I would have started over or tweaked my path. I'd have been more clear on why I was doing it. I would have been more introspective *and* asked for more guidance/help from other people, and I definitely would have made sure my actions were more meaningful. Ha! I would have done what I'm suggesting you do by following the Mind-Morph Way!

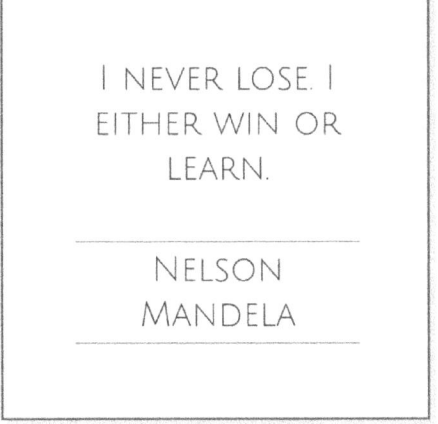

Resetting Techniques

Sometimes, resetting involves only awareness. You might take a mental look at the progress toward your Morph-Star and recognize that you are not where you want to be or moving in the right direction. Keeping a growth mindset, be sure to project this as an absolute positive – "I'm not satisfied with what I've done so far, so I'm going to try another way." Resetting is not a failure. Heck! Even if the reset means not continuing forward with your initial desire, that decision/action is not a failure. It is learning. It is growing. It is conscious awareness and choice to continue to strive for your life-change – perhaps in a different way.

Sometimes, you may be happy with actions and progress, although perhaps not everything. Here again, stop what you feel is not working and continue to pursue those actions providing better results. The process of quickly ending futile actions to embrace actions of progress embodies the Thomas Edison adage, "I have not failed. I've just found 10,000 ways that won't work." A great example of a growth mindset.

Think through and follow only the items listed here, which you feel you need as you choose to *reset*.

- **STOP!**

    The first step in resetting is to stop what you are doing now. Stop everything. Stop thinking/overthinking, put the brakes on any actions which are in progress, stop telling people about your dreams (for now). Just stop everything associated with your Morph-Star.

- **Check the *why*.**

  Remind yourself of why you want to achieve the life-change desire you have chosen. Make sure it reflects who you are as a person and your beliefs.

- **Ask (again).**

  Be sure to ask God or your Higher Power again about whether your life-change desire is a worthy pursuit for you at this time. If you have not yet, ask for honest feedback from someone you trust about what you are doing. It may not be what you want to hear, but an outside perspective can offer clarity when you most need it.

- **Redo your action list.**

  Without looking at your previous action list, re-list the actions you feel like you need to be taking on a clean, fresh piece of paper. For each one, try and get as detailed as you can about what is needed, who can assist, and how to accomplish it. Taking a new approach to your action list will often open an avenue of thinking you may not have had before. Your plan and organizational system go hand-in-hand with your action list, so check or redo those.

- **Change it up!**

  Consider a change-up. Sometimes a change of scenery helps as a part of the reboot. Work from the local coffee shop or library instead of your home office, move the furniture around in your office or take that much-needed vacation.

- **Rethink your support system.**

   One of the hardest things to do when making solid life-changes, is getting good support. Often, we think we are strong enough to "go it alone." Personal experience tells me it is a hard thing to do. If everyone around you is trying to hold you back, this can slow or even stop your progress. Make sure you are interfacing on a daily/regular basis with like-minded individuals who believe in you and your desire as much as you do.

- **Meditate.**

   Give yourself time to be thoughtful about what you're doing. Pray about it. Meditate on it, not necessarily thinking through your action items, but considering the scope of your desire, and what that desire means for you, your family, the people in your Circles, and your life. Meditate as if it has already happened, i.e., ask yourself and think through the energy you receive around questions such as "Is this right for me?" or "Should I be doing this right now?"

- **Journal.**

   Write out how you want your life to look as a result of this change. Explain the feelings you have as you think of how life will be when you have achieved your Morph-Star. Every time you embrace that feeling, your mind begins to turn the feeling into a habit, and this will serve to drive you to your desire.

- **Do a check-in.**

Before you do a reset, take a quick, mental inventory to determine what is working and what is not working. Life change or big life undertakings can be overwhelming. Make sure you have an understanding as to the actions which are positive and working for you.

- **Restart!**

Once you've explored these items, if you feel like you need to, then get back to it. Cycle back to Section A of the ABCs where you left off and pick it back up.

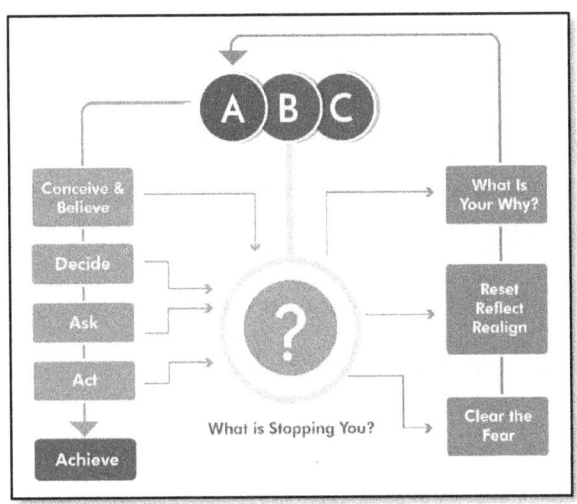

When considering a complete reset, there are two points of certainty worth seeking:

> 1) Does your Morph-Star match your personal, spiritual, and universal *beliefs*? Remember, there's nothing wrong with having personal wealth. Being wealthy simply for the sake of being the *one with the most* is where problems start.
>
> 2) Do the *actions* you are taking match your personal, spiritual, and universal beliefs? For example, you may have a sincere desire to achieve personal wealth so you can engage in building churches in underprivileged areas. However, if to achieve the personal wealth you do something illegal or take advantage of unsuspecting customers, your efforts will almost certainly fail.

If your Morph-Star and your actions follow your beliefs, and your beliefs are aligned (as I describe later), then resetting your action may be all you need to do.

You can rock your life-change and desire! Resetting is often a fundamental part of the process, not an end.

Reflect

Unlike resetting, where you're likely to stop and restart, reflecting is more about careful concentration and focus throughout your life-change adventure.

Reflecting is what I should have done more often each time I wanted to realize a new dream. Reflecting can be a hard thing for those of us who like to multitask and process information quickly. We are more about the *go* and less about the slow-down-and-think-this-through, and there are advantages to both of those characteristics. Reflecting needs to be done each time you Mind-Morph.

Reflecting Techniques

Reflecting can be considered the *meditate* step we just outlined in resetting. Although you may not be meditating on whether you should or should not be making this current life-change or seeking this particular desire, you will want to be thoughtful – meditative – about each portion of the Mind-Morph Mechanism. (While we are talking about getting out of Section B of the ABCs here, it is a good idea to be especially reflective during the process of taking actions toward your achievement.)

- **Find some quiet time.**
  If the needle seems like it has stopped moving for you, try and find some quiet time to go over where you are along the path. Quiet time means a complete disconnect – I know, I know! Trust me, you can survive without your phone, computer or tablet for a couple of hours. When you cut the cord, you may find that your creativity level starts going way up. Quiet time is different than meditating. Start by trying not to think about your Morph-Star. If you find your thoughts drifting back to it without creating stress, then go with the flow.
- **Remind yourself.**
  Remind yourself not why you started this life- change,

rather how it feels once you achieve it. Sink yourself into your imagination about how great your clothes fit when you lose that weight, or how much love you feel when you find someone special or how much confidence you will have when you land the perfect job. Don't forget the true result (fulfillment of your *why*) by reaching your achievement and desire. Do you need to write an affirmation as a reminder of the greatness that will come?

- **Think through your actions.**

  Regularly, and especially if your process has slowed, block off some quality thinking time for your action items. It is good to consider these in two contexts: the completeness and accuracy of your action list and whether you are following through on completing them.

- **Refine.**

  One of the greatest benefits of continually reflecting is the refining process that occurs in our brains. The more we think about something, the more we learn it. The more we learn it, the more our brains scan the details, find efficiencies, and expose potential risks. Then we think through those areas and refine again. Reflecting can feel like a slowdown when we start to get attached to our plans and close to our actions. This is often a time when the brain is refining, quietly, in the background. If you find yourself here, think through any actions that may be coming up for you. If that feels comfortable, make a list of the action items you think of as part of your refining process.

- **Reflect through adversity.**
  There is an old Chinese proverb that says something like, "When you've gone down 90% of the road, you're halfway to your destination." If you've ever been involved in a major project, as silly as this logic sounds, you know it to be true. Sometimes it just feels like we're ready to scream out, "Why can't I just finish this!" Those are the times to reflect through all you have accomplished.

- **Celebrate!**
  Celebrate your progress and embrace the fact you are nearly complete! Fist pump, lift your hands in the air as a proclamation of personal victory or chest-bump the person closest to you! Definitely celebrate. We can be hardest on and have the highest expectations for ourselves, so we need time to enjoy our progress. You might consider making a list of achievements to look back on.

Realign

Realigning means what it says: Get back into alignment. Have you ever driven a car that needs a front-end alignment? You can point the car straight ahead, and if you take your hands off the steering wheel, the car will immediately stray to the left or right. The faster it moves to one side or the other, the worse the alignment is.

> LORD KNOWS, EVERY DAY IS NOT A SUCCESS, EVERY YEAR IS NOT A SUCCESS. YOU HAVE TO CELEBRATE THE GOOD.
>
> REESE WITHERSPOON

Wandering out of alignment is one of the most common reasons we lose progress in our efforts. One of the reasons misalignment is such a challenge is because it can occur in any *one,* or *many,* of the areas we are working. When we talk about being out of alignment, think of it in terms of when you have a feeling of being *off* or out-of-sorts with something or someone around you. I am fond of saying, "My mojo is off today" for those times when it seems like nothing is going my way. I'm hitting all of the red lights; I'm calling a bunch of people, though no one is available; or I've offended someone, and I'm not even sure how.

You may have heard the term *the planets are all lined up* when someone is referring to a big thing happening in their lives. That's where we want to be, except a lot more often and around everything we are doing. When you check your alignment you'll want to check:

- ✓ Are you in alignment with your beliefs? – These are your desires, your thoughts, your actions in agreement with what you believe to be right and good.
- ✓ Are you in alignment with those around you? What are your thoughts and behaviors towards all people?
- ✓ Are your beliefs in alignment with your family, society, your community?
- ✓ Are your actions in alignment with the universe around you – are you moving in the same direction? (Are you following the "flow" of life?) Alignment can sometimes be a strong feeling – like the easy sway of a gentle wind.
- ✓ Are you deflecting negative energy, so it has no (zero) hold on you?
- ✓ Are you projecting the positive – passing smiles to strangers, giving of your time and talent, offering uplifting and encouraging words?
- ✓ Are you receiving positive information from all sources, i.e., social media, TV, radio, news, support network?

Realigning Techniques

When you feel like you aren't in alignment, there are many ways to realign. It's kind of like going to a chiropractor – when you do it, you feel soooo much better when you leave. And you feel even better the more you go. It's the same feeling here. When you realign, you are going to feel awesome again! You will feel even better each time you realign. Do it often. There is no such thing as being *overly* aligned.

- **Take care of yourself!**

    Taking care of yourself may seem or sound like a simple thing, though we don't often take time to do it. When was the last time you pampered yourself? Took some time off just for yourself? Or are you spending money on yourself instead of your kids? What are three things that bring you joy, and how can you do one this week?

- **Get into a good space.**

    Getting into a good space is a little different than taking care of yourself. This action can is more like relaxing your mind. We are typically our own worst critics and can be a bit hard on ourselves. Give yourself permission to take a break – spend time on yourself for an hour or take a day off. Stress causes a lot of misalignment, so take some time to get your head on straight and think clearly. Even if you don't need this right now, take a moment to jot down what works best for you for stress relief.

- **Forgive/Release**

    When your mind and thoughts are fixed on other people or any of the various situations in your life, the same "get into a good space" principle applies. If you're feeling anger or resentment toward someone or if you are not happy with situations in and around your life, that negative mindset will also cause misalignment. Think about what works for you and what energizes you into positive thinking and positive reactions/responses to this type of adversity. Permit yourself to *let go* of this negativity.

- **Take comfort in your *why*.**

    You may, at times question and re-question why you've decided to make this change or fulfill your desire. It is common to begin talking yourself out of your decision after you've committed and started – especially if you're facing some adversity. Again, if your *why* is sincere and right for you, then keep embracing it. You might need to remind yourself that you are happy with why you are changing. If you feel like you might have the wrong why, check out the exercises in <u>Finding My Why</u> in the Supplement section of the book.

- **Have some patience…**

    If you are anything like me, you want all these great things for yourself and your family fulfilled *right now*. If there is one thing I have figured out, it is that all things will come in their due time. No matter how hard we press it (or even try to force it), the Universe has this way of working perfectly, which includes making things happen right when they should. Have some patience with the workings of the Universe, energy and spiritual power.

- **Does it feel forced?**

    If feeling like you are working hard and/or forcing something to happen are symptoms of being out of alignment for you, that may be the time to back off a bit and regroup. Relax your action items and work on clearing your mind of the clutter. When it's right, things will start to *click*.

These are just a few of the realignment techniques which will help you to regain your focus, effort, and energy around fulfilling your desires for an abundant life. Think about the ways that work best for you. What helps you to get your thoughts and ideas – your frame of mind – into a clear, positive, forward-moving state? It can be as easy as spending time in the garden,

> IF YOU ARE IN ALIGNMENT, LIFE CAN BE EASY.

relaxing on the beach listening to the ocean, putting your earbuds in, and taking a run or walking through the neighborhood park. What gets you into your *zone*?

Consistently living in the zone is the mind-change; this is the change of life. To live it fully, consider how often you are prayerful (asking) about everything in which you are engaged. If you are in alignment, life CAN be easy – it all falls into place.

R-R-R Remedies

During those times when you are living the Three R's – Reset, Reflect, Realign – I have found these remedies to be effective for assisting with the process of regrouping and getting your mind and thinking back to your chosen path.

These remedies don't require much effort. I think you will find them to be quite sobering, a way for you to gain perspective and discover your true priorities.

Gratitude

I often say we need to adopt an "attitude of gratitude." Too many times, we concentrate on what we don't have, what isn't working, or why we aren't "successful" – *fixed mindset*. What we should be doing is showing sincere appreciation for all we do have – a *growth mindset*.

If you woke up this morning in your bed, you are already

better rested than any of the estimated 100 million people who are homeless in the world. If you were able to eat breakfast, then you are kick-starting your day in a way that approximately 815 million people globally are not able to. If you have a job, you can enjoy the security and benefits employment provides, which more than 192 million people around the world will hope for today. This is a small sampling of what most of us *have* in life. For what else do *you* have to be grateful? List three things right now:

1. _____
2. _____
3. _____

It is also impossible to be simultaneously grateful and fearful. When we are engaged in thanksgiving, our minds override selfish thoughts and feelings to create space for humility and to take stock of our abundance.

Be sure to thank God or your Higher Power for what you have during your time of prayer or meditation. Discuss your blessings with your family or members of your congregation. Choose one way you can give back or pay it forward.

Service

I have been given (and have offered others) the counsel to "serve in times of need or despair." It's important to serve *often*, and especially during times of difficulty. There is little else that will facilitate clarity, as well as uplift your mood and thoughts surrounding your situation, than serving someone else in greater need than you. This effort doesn't need to be large scale. Holding the door open for other people walking into the grocery store, paying for lunch at the drive-thru for the car behind you, or listening to a friend who may be struggling with a life challenge are all excellent ways of serving.

There are likely several ways you can further serve in non-profit organizations in your community, join in community service projects with your teenagers, and offer your time and talent for needy church members of your congregation.

I can say it no more clearly than this – service works when it comes to resetting, reflecting, and realigning!

Inspired Action

There is a difference between *inspiration* and ***inspired action***. Inspiration is that rush of adrenalin that flows through you when you hear a speaker, see a movie or video or read a story with a message that resonates with you so deeply, you feel like you want to jump in and do something right at the moment. I get this way after I watch any of the *Rocky* movies. Even though Rocky Balboa is a boxer, when he overcomes his adversary – which, by the way, is usually more personal than physical – I feel inspired that I can overcome my adversaries too!

An *inspired* action is when you feel compelled to take specific actions as a result of certain, usually personal, inspirations. That feeling is the inspiration that will sometimes come to you in the middle of the night when you bolt wide awake and think, "Oh my gosh, this is a great idea!" I believe these inklings are nestled into your subconscious and make themselves known to you at times when you are in your deepest, clearest thought, meditation, prayer, and silent consideration. More often they need silence and solitude to surface – which is one reason they happen while we sleep, among the many other places this phenomenon can occur.

Begin the process of finding what helps you get into these types of clear-thought periods. It will likely take some practice. As you get better at having clear, open thinking episodes at a conscious level, you will increase your ability to harness an amazing mind-changing superpower.

Setback or Set UP?

Several times throughout the book, I've emphasized how we condition into habits that hinder our personal growth and limit our beliefs. Just as believing you've failed at something (when you've only experienced a learning opportunity), believing you've had a "setback" on your mind-change journey is a limiting belief.

When you live the Mind-Morph Way, you will begin to

believe that what appears to be a setback is more of a *set UP*. The event that seems to set you back is setting you up for your next big step. For example, friends of mine – a married couple with children – were preparing for a big move as part of a new job my friend was taking in another state. The job was not his "dream job," though he was excited about the opportunity. Everything seemed to be moving perfectly through the process, and you could say he was well-aligned.

Then, in the final week or so before the move, the situation with their new home fell through, and they were back at the beginning of searching for a place to live. My friend was supposed to start his new job the following week. Panic set in as they began to search for a new home frantically. My friend was worried he wouldn't be allowed to keep the job if he had not moved, and he couldn't afford a temporary solution such as staying in a hotel in the new city. I remember hearing his wife describe the situation to some other ladies at a church function by saying, "We've had a major setback in our move." And for all intents and purposes, this appeared to be a pretty major setback.

While this was all going on, my friend did something that might have been considered unthinkable by those around him. He took some time away, making a 10-hour drive to spend some spiritual time alone. He felt he needed to ask God, the Universe, and himself about all that was going on. He needed time to privately, inwardly reflect and realign. As he concluded his spiritual hiatus, he confided in me that he felt fairly peaceful despite the circumstances.

He also felt inspired to reach out to a company he'd worked with in the past and which he reluctantly left despite his passion for working there. He made the call, and the timing couldn't have been better for him. A position in his former department was open, he was qualified, and the pay and benefits were better than the new job he was preparing to take. This job would still require a move, however there were multiple homes on the market within a short distance of the office.

Within about 10 days, my friend's life went from chaos to fulfilling a life-change desire. What was initially a setback turned out to be a set up for what he wanted all along.

Your perspective – how you look through (and past) a situation – will largely determine whether you respond to it as a setback or as it legitimately is: a set UP for something better.

The Science

It breaks my heart when I hear people repeat phrases they consider to be truths about personal growth.
"You have to work hard to get ahead,"
"Fight for what you want," or
"No pain, no gain."

We've all heard, and said, similar sentiments. These concepts are not true. And, it is dangerous for us to adopt them as beliefs.

If you compare exercising; 1. behavioral characteristics surrounding what you believe; 2. the mental attitude you adopt when acting toward life fulfillment; and 3. how you respond to change or adversity, with exercising your physical body, you will see that you can reach the same results, if not better results, without pain, agony, or weight room grunting.

When working out the body to build strength or stamina, the result of that workout should not be to feel pain. If you feel pain during or after a physical workout, your body is telling you, "I need to rest." If you work through the pain or endure it for days after your workout, you are doing nothing more than subjecting yourself to needless self-suffering.

The same can be said when you endure day-after-day financial struggle, addiction, mental or physical abuse, and/or drudgery at work. You are only subjecting yourself to needless self-suffering because life CAN be different if you exercise your change of mind correctly.

Even when performed correctly, you may still experience some discomfort – in your physical workout or your mind-change workout. Discomfort is much different than pain. When you remain present during uncomfortable moments, that's when the physical body is building muscle and endurance and when your mental muscles are adapting and changing for the *better*! For example, there are extraordinary benefits in performing Tai Chi – an ancient Chinese art of embracing mind, body, and spirit, somewhat similar to Yoga. Tai Chi combines slow, graceful movements and controlled breathing to cultivate internal life energy and invite it to flow smoothly, yet powerfully, throughout the body. A growing number of studies show increased health, function, strength and emotional, as well as physical, life quality by those who regularly practice the art of Tai Chi. *No* pain and ***plenty of gains*** – at the mental, physical and metaphysical/universal states.

"Recalibrate" – The Final R

Ultimately, resetting, reflecting, and realigning are different ways of *recalibrating*. To calibrate something, you measure its current state against a point of reference. Typically, the point of reference is the correct setting for the item you are calibrating.

For example, a factory makes pancakes (yummy!) and uses a special device that pours exactly 1/4 cup of batter for each pancake. Every 100 pancakes, the pouring device is tested to make certain it is still pouring exactly 1/4 cup of batter. If it is not, recalibration adjustments are in the form of cleaning, nozzle adjustments, or consistency of the batter. Recalibration is needed from time-to-time to make certain the pancake machine stays as accurate, and on-track to meet the goal of producing the required number of pancakes.

It is not at all uncommon for us to need to check ourselves to make sure we are also on-track toward our goals. Even though I feel like I have a pretty good handle on my finances, I recently opened a blank spreadsheet and started going through my bank and credit card statements. In the spreadsheet, I recorded the days of the month my regular payments deduct from my accounts. Sure enough, I found a couple of monthly subscription payments I had intended to cancel and had forgotten. I adjusted the current state of my spending against a point of reference indicating where they should be aligned. That's recalibrating.

The more you check yourself, and recalibrate, the more real your Morph-Star feels. The closer it feels, and the more you build that conscious and subconscious desire to keep reaching for the prize. Keep affirming, and reminding yourself that <u>you can</u>, <u>you will</u>, and <u>you are</u> **going to reach your desire!**

Your Mind-Point

Where are you at this point in your Mind-Morph journey? Do you need to reset, reflect, realign or recalibrate? Check your Mind-Point for some inspiration.

You may feel like you are living in a state of resetting, however you are not. Be aware that you may possess a heightened tendency to have a critical view of yourself, your journey, and your ability to reach your life-change desire. Now is the time to work through that discomfort, without letting it become painful. Understand you may be taking on some new thought patterns and perspectives and certainly taking action you might not have taken before. You are Mind-Morphing! Keep going because you are almost there! Your action item here is to hold fast to your Morph-Star and take that next critical step toward reaching your ideal life.

Diamonds, you may not be as self-critical as Traingles, but you will be tempted to let yourself off-the-hook when you start to get outside your comfort zone. When that happens, take the time to reflect. Recall the reasons you started this journey. Look back at the answers you've recorded in this book and reaffirm them or adjust to what feels right for you. Once you're feeling invigorated again, step back into your actions and take yourself to a new, expanded comfort zone. When you do that, you will know everything you are working toward is within your reach.

"Realign, realign, realign" should be your new mantra. While tasks and projects may flow easily for you when it comes to changing how you think, you may find yourself straying off course and digging yourself into something you can do without having to change. I will remind you that your Morph-Star may not be easy, however it will be 100% worth it. Check-in with yourself and remind yourself that you are capable of doing (and *want* to do) this thing. As I mentioned earlier in this chapter, consider taking up Yoga or Tai Chi – great ways to align your body, mind, and spirit and invite all things in your universe to flow as nicely as your work projects.

Squares, there is a song by Little River Band with lyrics that say, in portion,
"Take time to make time,
Make time to be there.
Look around, be a part..."

As you move through your actions, sometimes you may feel like you are taking one step forward and two steps back. That will occur regardless of the thing for which you are striving. As the song goes – be there. Be a part. Enjoy the experience of it all. Anxiety and fear are natural mental "pains." We don't want the pain, so take time to reflect. Be in this moment with the universe, keep asking for direction from God or your Higher Power, and go with it. In the end, if you stay the course, it will come. Read your affirmation(s) aloud, and begin your next step toward fulfilling your Morph-Star.

Take Time Now to Reset, Reflect, Realign

In which ways would resetting your Morph-Star affect your results?

_____
_____
_____
_____

Reflect on your Morph-Star and describe why it is still important to you.

_____
_____
_____
_____

As you reflect, write down the benefits of taking time away from your actions.

_____
_____
_____
_____

Capture some of the ways you feel you are out of alignment in your life right now.

_____

_____
_____
_____

Choose the one thing most out of alignment for you and write down what you need to do to bring it back into alignment. (Refer to the tips in this chapter).

_____
_____
_____
_____

As a reminder to yourself, write down what it feels like (will feel like) once you have achieved your Morph-Star.

_____
_____
_____
_____

A True Story About Resetting

During high school, our friend began working his first real, paying job. He now has experiences with people that have money and can afford better things – new clothes, being able to go out to movies/restaurants, and even cars. He recognizes that he isn't going to get any of these items from wealthy parents. He can work for these items on his own, and he starts by flipping hamburgers at age 15.

He is practicing his new mindset – that he can rise above adversity and his present circumstances – he better handles his thoughts and reactions to difficult situations at school and work. He adopts a "take it head-on" philosophy as challenges arise. Various situational experiences and his continued upbringing of his brother and sister set him on his life path. His experiences of resetting plans and actions which don't pan out as expected, reflecting on building positive momentum, and continually realigning set a standard by which he lives his adult life.

Resetting and realigning become an all-too-common theme as he approaches and moves into adulthood. He experiences every bit of the up and down cycle of life as most of us know it. He is married and divorced twice, files for bankruptcy, and experiences the humiliation of car repossession, eviction, and home foreclosure. He lives as most of us live our lives – some good times and many bad times. Having developed a love of business, he operates a small computer consultancy with moderate success. He goes on to execute on various business dealings and claims to this day that he's had many more failures than successes, although he now sees the perfection and learning through those failures.

In one such instance, he experiences an extremely difficult business transaction. This situation culminated in a heavy, personal financial loss, instability in his personal life among family and friends, and an emotional low point he had never before experienced.

After one particular phone call, which revealed the extent of the damage from the situation, he hung up the phone, thinking there was no way his position could be any worse. It was in this moment of ultimate despair and the emotional crisis he sat alone and speaking aloud proclaimed, "I will not give up! I will not deny the power of God! You can drive me down as much as you want, and I will not give up!" It was, indeed, a time for him to reset, reflect and realign nearly the entirety of what his life had been for the previous three years. And so, for another time in his life, a new journey began for him – one which would require his greatest mind-change ever.

To be concluded...

📍 MIND-MORPH JOURNEY
RESET, REFLECT, REALIGN

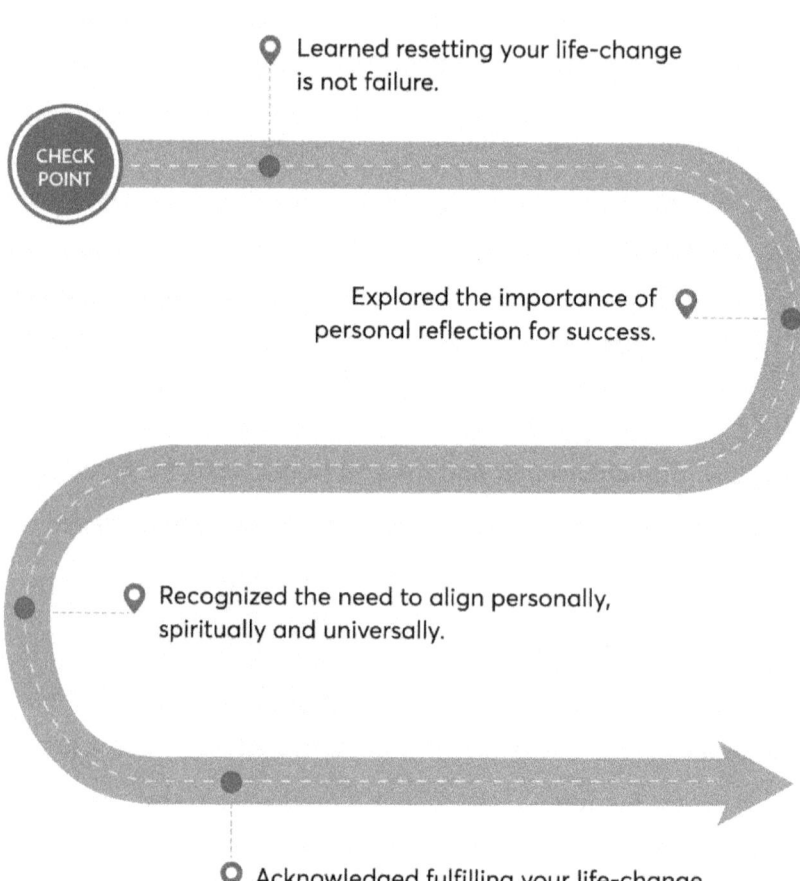

- Learned resetting your life-change is not failure.
- Explored the importance of personal reflection for success.
- Recognized the need to align personally, spiritually and universally.
- Acknowledged fulfilling your life-change does not need to be a painful process.

CHECK POINT

Copyright © Chris Doyle, Mind-Morph

Chapter 8
A Key to the Universe

"When you want something, all the universe conspires in helping you to achieve it."
Paulo Coelho

One of my favorite activities is trying to get out of an escape room. The escape room experience places you inside a locked room, designed to make getting out difficult. You have a limited amount of time to solve a series of puzzles and riddles, overcoming various challenges that uncover clues to the key that will unlock a final door leading to freedom.

Sometimes you find yourself struggling to get out. You just aren't seeing the clues in front of you. Even when you slow down, they can still be difficult to find. If you don't make it out of the room in the allotted time, a guide comes in and shows you the solution for each portion of the escape. It is with the guide's assistance when you get the eye-opening, "I-can't-believe-I-didn't-see-that" awareness. The troubling part is realizing how easy it would have been to get out once you see the solution.

Unfiltered awareness is the feeling you will have when you experience the Mind-Morph Mechanism working for you the first (or second) time. Each time it works, it will become easier and easier for you to fix upon your next Morph-Star, believe you can achieve it, and take the actions to fulfill your deepest desires. The ultimate "ah-ha" is realizing that the *key* to all of this is, quite simply – **you**! You represent the *Master Key* and all of the tips, tools, and techniques presented in this book are **keys** you use to unlock your potential and various opportunities. There are many more keys in the Universe as well, just waiting to be found and used.

Living Intentionally

While you will use the Mind-Morph Mechanism independently for your each of your Morph-Stars, the Mind-Morph Way should become more of a lifestyle. It is a manner of proactive, intentional living and creating your everyday life. When you live Mind-Morph, you take complete ownership of the *new you* and continually develop your habits for success.

Like exercising the muscles in your body, exercising the muscle in your mind – living the Mind-Morph Way – takes practice. As physical exercise requires a daily routine, so does mind-change. Intentionally considering "how I think," "how I live" and "how I work" must remain a constant action item until it becomes second nature to you – a habit.

Though I was not necessarily practicing Mind-Morph (I

hadn't thought of it yet), when I was 19 years old, I set a goal for myself to earn $100,000 by the time I was 30 years old. I had met that income level by the time I was 25. I then raised that expectation to $200,000 by the time I was 30 and exceeded that by almost $25,000. Recognizing this pattern of setting goals beyond what I *thought* I could achieve, my new goal is to earn one million dollars, and I am on my way!

"It was a lot of work but I'm creating an environment of intentional living."

The Science

It can be difficult to overcome a lifetime of negativity or non-belief to change your life for the better. Such change takes time, patience and repeated realignment. In his book, *Outliers,* Malcolm Gladwell discusses what he calls the "10,000 Hour Rule." Essentially, the 10,000 Hour Rule says it takes 10,000 hours of deliberate practice to become "world-class" in something. For those of us that can't easily perform complex math – 10,000 hours is equivalent to 417, 24-hour days. If you were to dedicate 8 hours per day, 10,000 hours would amount to roughly 3.5 years. Gladwell cautions against oversimplifying his concept. Several other factors come into play if you are striving to become a world-class musician, for example. You can see that whatever you choose to engage in will take deliberate practice and daily consciousness. Your challenge is to practice Mind-Morph for 10,000 hours!

Not only do we need to continue practicing the totality of the Mind-Morph Mechanism, we also need to stay in a positive environment and positive frame of mind as often as possible. It makes logical sense if we have someone (or many people) around us who do not support our life-change efforts, we will be less successful, or not successful at all. Barbara Fredrickson, a professor in the Psychology Department at the University of North Carolina, has published several materials about the actual science behind the power of positive thought (or positive signaling as we know it in Mind-Morph).

Take, for example, the scenario where you and an office mate are in the break room at work smiling, laughing, and having a great discussion about what you were doing over the weekend. Then, someone comes into the break room, slams the door, mumbles something under their breath, and proceeds over to the coffee machine. The weight of the negative signaling that just came into the room is now hovering over everyone. You and your friend stop your conversation, stop laughing and your smiles completely disappear.

In her book, *Positivity*, Professor Fredrickson shows that those negative signals are, in fact, three times more powerful than positive signals. That means for you and your office mate to get back to the great mood you were in before the door-slamming, under-the-breath-mumbling incident in the break room; you will need to experience three positive events or actions.

Not only that, Dr. Fredrickson goes on to describe how the effects of positive influences impact the brain to provide much more than just happiness. Positivity promotes overall joy and gratitude and broadens the mind so it will open up to new possibilities and ideas. Positivity is especially important during the growth process of mind-change, such as in Mind-Morph, because the brain remembers, reacts and more readily recalls bad things which have occurred

> ONCE YOU REPLACE NEGATIVE THOUGHTS WITH POSITIVE ONES, YOU'LL START HAVING POSITIVE RESULTS.
>
> WILLIE NELSON

in our lives. An example of this could be if we were living in a jungle, knowing a lion could eat us at any moment. The brain reacts to this by creating a survival instinct, constantly remembering this negative possibility. To overcome that negative, a factor of three positives need to be present. If we draw this back into something in our everyday lives, the *lion* is present in the form of poverty, abuse, and addiction, to name a few of the everyday negatives that may plague us.

Gratefully, we now know, through the Mind-Morph Way, we have absolute control over all these situations and can *create* the abundant life we most deeply desire. And, as part of the Mind-Morph Way, we surround ourselves with positive people and adopt a growth mindset.

Considering we need a three-to-one ratio of positive influences to negative, here are some ways (additional keys to add to your keychain) to keep positive energy flowing daily:

Staying Positive

- **Keep your media positive.** Radio, TV, and social media should make you feel good about yourself and the world around you. If it does not, then turn it off, change the station, or remove negative posts/friends from your news feeds.
- **Send positive signals.** When you give positive, you get

positive back. Smile at those around you, offer small gestures such as paying for a cup of coffee or holding a door open. Offer uplifting and encouraging words for others who may be in a bad mood today.

- **Enjoy positive friends.** Other people may not be Mind-Morphing the way you are. They can still offer support or overall friendliness. Surround yourself with these types of people at all levels of your day-to-day life.
- **Control your response.** Not everything that happens in life is necessarily a positive event. Find the good in it. Find the humor in a difficult situation. Choose not to respond negatively, rather in a positive fashion regardless of who may be at fault or what the challenge is.

A New Universal Perspective

As you begin to *live* Mind-Morph, you will find that you are living a completely new perspective. Perhaps one you hadn't previously thought of or thought possible. You will also be living your new perspective consistently – daily. It will not be a manufactured difference in life, such as a difficult diet quickly abandoned. Rather, it will be a natural change of life and mind easily sustained.

The old perspective can is in the diagram below. It is one where you exist under these circumstances:

The Old Way of Thinking

- All things occur within the scope of the Universe.
- You use various laws at various times in anticipation of generating a potential result or outcome. For example,
    - You signal to the Universe how badly you would like something.
    - You plead with your Higher Power to deliver it to you.
    - You press people and processes with hopes of forcing it into being.
- As a result, a small percentage of time these efforts work, and you celebrate a victory.
- This way is not a consistent, sustainable or even desirable method.

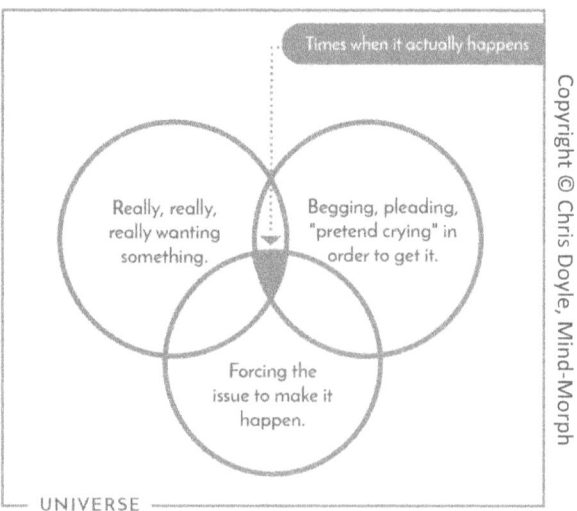

The New Way of Thinking

- All things occur within the scope of Spiritual Law – God or your Higher Power.
- You believe the Universe will align with your subconscious and use Buckets of Laws to create your ideal life.
- You understand purpose and perfection in all things.
- You consistently create positive opportunities.
- You are at peace if you do not obtain a desire and seek other opportunities.
- This way creates a more desirable path, a repeatable mechanism, and a life of fulfilled desire.

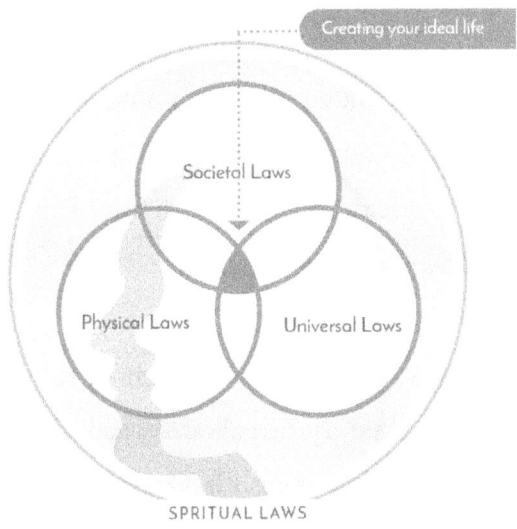

Copyright © Chris Doyle, Mind-Morph

Mind-Morphed

Most of us have heard the stories of well-known people who have overcome tremendous life challenges and achieved greatness in their respective fields. Though they were not practicing Mind-Morph, I would say they have Mind-Morphed. They changed their way of thinking away from what might be a stereotype into a mindset of achievement and success. At one time in their lives, they *flipped the switch*. Some of the more well-known ones are:

Oprah Winfrey – A survivor of childhood sexual abuse; was a runaway and the teenaged mother of a child who died shortly after birth. She is now a billionaire and extremely successful businesswoman with several businesses.

J.K Rowling – Single mother living in poverty who experienced rejection of her books hundreds of times; at one point in her life, she contemplated suicide. She is the author of the *Harry Potter* book series and owner of the franchise.

Richard Branson – Did not do well in school and was labeled as lazy and ignorant. He has dyslexia and learned how to adapt to the condition. He owns and operates his Virgin Group empire which has a net worth of over 7 billion dollars.

Have you heard of these people who also overcame extreme

difficulties to fulfill their desires?

Curtis Jackson – He was to a teenage mother who was murdered when he was 8 years old. By the time he turned 15, he had dropped out of school, bought a gun and started dealing drugs. He spent several years in and out of jail and was shot – and survived – nine times. You may know him as 50 Cent, a leader in the hip-hop community who has pursued other interests such as television production.

Melissa Stockwell – Lost her leg in a roadside bomb attack while she was serving in the U.S. Military in Iraq. Refusing to let her disability hold her back, she's earned several swimming records while participating in the Paralympics and is now a triathlon coach.

Kris Carr – Went from struggling entertainer and photographer to highly successful healthy lifestyle expert. After being diagnosed with a rare type of cancer, she wrote the *Crazy Sexy Cancer* book, which turned into a documentary on TLC. That success inspired her to start the popular website my.crazysexylife.com. She continues to write and promote healthy living despite challenges that might hold other people back.

One thing all of these people have in common is they are just exactly like you and me! They have also morphed their minds, followed their Morph-Stars and achieved life abundance, and this is just a small sample of individual accomplishments. Many, many people have done it. Think about all the people you may know who have changed their lives to achieve success in some particular endeavor. How about you?

Each of these people had different Morph-Stars, and their journeys were different from each other. Their journeys are different from yours. Your journey is different from mine. Mind-Morph is a multifaceted approach; we are all multifaceted; problems are multifaceted, and life is multifaceted. That's what this is all about – use the Mind-Morph Mechanism in a way that best suits your desires and abilities to achieve success. However, you define it. That's what I did, and as I often say, "If *I* can do it, *anyone* can do it!"

If you change your mind,
you will change your life!

Your Mind-Point

You've got this! I know it may seem like some of this goes against all of your old conditioning. If you get yourself started and use the guide I've given you here, I have no doubt you will reach every level of success you want. Stephen R. Covey said, "There are three constants in life…change, choice, and principles." Choice and principles are already strong with you. Now embrace your Morph-Stars – the change Covey refers to as a constant. I believe in your ability to change your mind and your life!

You don't need to follow someone else or wait for others to show you the way, Yellow. Follow your Morph-Star; take hold, and do it! You may have some ups and downs. Reset, reflect and realign if that occurs and keep going. Don't lose sight of your ultimate achievement, and you will reach it. I believe anything you set your mind to; you can accomplish!

Your ability to conceive and believe has likely already started you down the path to achievement, perhaps chasing many dreams and desires. Keep your priorities in order, maintain life balance, and continue realigning. It will not be possible to achieve greatness in all things at once. You can achieve greatness in all things in their due order and time. Live life and be great!

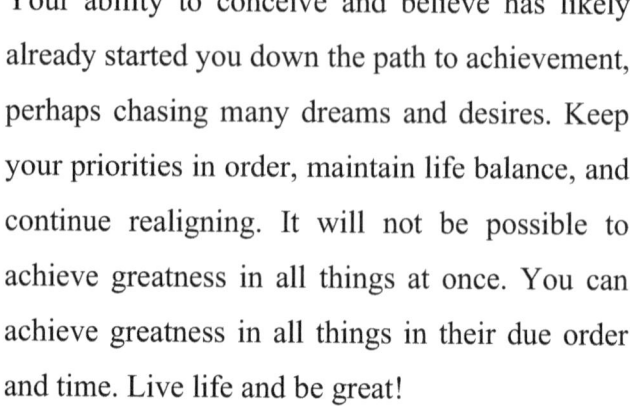
Your passion and positive living may give you a hint that all things are possible. And they are. Passion and positive thoughts are only effective when combined with positive action. Positive actions yield success in some way regardless of outcomes. That, in and of itself, is an achievement. When you put it all together – belief, decision, asking and action – you are *unstoppable*!

Mind Your Morph

Imagine you have fulfilled your Morph-Star! You've done it! Tell me what it's like – how does your achievement look and feel?

_____
_____
_____
_____

Describe what you will do to celebrate your success. With who will you share? How will you reflect on your journey to achievement?

_____
_____
_____
_____

The only thing greater than the fulfillment of a desire is sharing your journey. How will you share your story or help others reach their Morph-Star?

_____
_____
_____
_____

A True Story Concluded

I've been telling you a true story about a young man who grew up in poverty and struggled into his adult years.

This young man is *me*!

I share my story because I believe we all have these different turning points that occur in our lives. Some are apparent to us right away, and others aren't apparent until we reflect later, however each could represent a new chapter in our lives.

The boxing match in 5th grade was one of those turning points. No doubt it was a flip-the-switch moment for me. Each downtime ended a chapter as a new one started – my first divorce ended a difficult chapter, and started a happier new one. My second divorce ended a chapter (not nearly as difficult as the first one) and started a happier new one. When people see where I am today and ask me how I got here, what motivated me the most was the conclusion of that business transaction. It's hard to describe the difficulty of that period, and it was an absolute challenge, in every way.

Throughout my spiritual journey in life, I'd heard the story of the refiner's fire – a process that a metal worker goes through when making something like a sword, for example. To get the metal to its strongest form, its sharpest edge, its perfect shape, the swordsmith works the metal in and out of the fire multiple times. Into the blazing fire. Then out of the fire and pounded or folded and back into the fire. Out for more shaping, then back in. All of this until the sword is the shape the swordsmith wants before it is finally cooled, polished and finished. In the end, the metal comes out as a beautiful sword, even though the process was hard and arduous. Is this not the perfect analogy for life? Thrust into the fire during difficult times. Each time we come out, we are better – we are stronger, we are sharper, we are better than before. And so it goes.

When that ordeal was over for me, I resolved within myself that I would share my life-change, my mind-change so others could benefit from my experience. My hope is this message reaches many people – I would love for a billion people to hear it. Although, if even just *one* person can change their life, then I will feel I have achieved this Morph-Star of mine.

And, we are not at "the end" as the remainder of this story is yet to be created!

MIND-MORPH JOURNEY
A KEY TO THE UNIVERSE

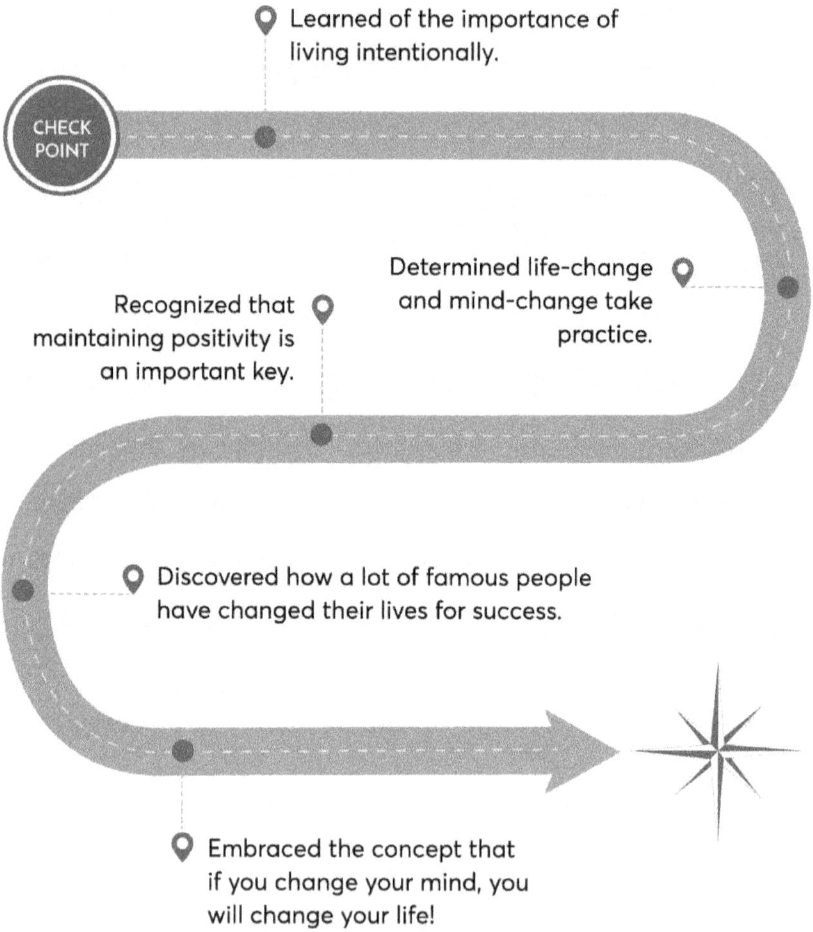

CHECK POINT

- Learned of the importance of living intentionally.
- Recognized that maintaining positivity is an important key.
- Determined life-change and mind-change take practice.
- Discovered how a lot of famous people have changed their lives for success.
- Embraced the concept that if you change your mind, you will change your life!

Copyright © Chris Doyle, Mind-Morph

Conclusion
It's a Wrap

"If you believe you can, you can!"
Chris Doyle

How to conclude a book intentionally designed to be a beginning – the *start* of something new; a change of thinking; of mindset; of life? It seems like a contradiction to me. While this may be the end of the book, do not treat this as *your* end. Treat it as your *start* (or your continuation) of all the great work you have put into the action portion of each chapter. Find, and maintain, hope in the many possibilities inherent in the Mind-Morph Way. Return often to your margin notes, reflections, and survey answers as you embrace all of your Morph-Stars and continually create your ideal life.

I am asked, "Why does it matter? Why should I care about creating an ideal life? Isn't idealism a concept outside my reach?" The question is individualized and personal. My first inclination is to offer a Mind-Morph answer – "If you believe it is outside your reach, then it is. If you *believe* you can achieve far-reaching goals, then you **can!**" That would be my first inclination as I draw awareness on a more personal level to the person asking.

I would argue the greater Mind-Morph significance is not the change in any single individual, rather the abundance of change realized by the multitude of individuals collectively. Consider it this way:

Let's say you start by making a small mind-change. Then, you make another and over some time another and another. You are changing your mind, and as importantly, you are changing your way of life. A colleague at work (perhaps not even known to you) has noticed something *different* about you. Not bad different. Good different. And good different in a way as to have made a positive impact. Now, she wants to change her way of life as well. She might even ask you what you've found or how you are doing it. Inspired by you, she sets about making the changes she most desires.

As the days and months continue, your colleague is making positive strides to such a point others notice and find she, too, has become an inspiration to those around her. You've sparked even more people within your circles of influence, and they have started a personal mind and change journey. Do you see the infinite magnitude of this simple message? It may start with you, although it doesn't stop with you. And when enough people have recognized the power they have to create the ideal life they have always wanted, why then it becomes a bona fide ***movement***. It is a movement with enough positive energy to cross a country and span a world.

The *why* in the question "Why does it matter?" is because it will positively change your life – the *greater* why is because it will, without a doubt, **change the world**.

What to Do Next

My parting advice to you is to keep yourself engaged in forward momentum. If you didn't complete the action sections of the chapters as you read, then go back and do them now. If you engaged in the process during your reading, then keep going.

When I first took up running for exercise, I was trying to build my endurance. A running partner once told me, no matter what you do during your run, don't stop running. Even if it seems like a really fast walk, keep your momentum. Because once you slow to a walk, it is twice as hard to get your pace back up.

The same applies to Mind-Morph. Even during times when you are resetting or reflecting, keep that positive, forward motion. Remind yourself of your why, read your affirmations, find a mentor or two, work on your life balance. Remember, it may take time, but does not have to be hard. I cannot overstate the power you have to *create* for the good of yourself and those around you.

To help, I provide all of the surveys and chapter action sections on my website at www.mind-morph.com. I also invite you to share your story, your progress, your Morph-Star, and your achievements with the Mind-Morph community and me. If you are active on Facebook or Twitter, use these hashtags:

#mylifetbdbyme – to share your vision, life changes, affirmations, and Morph-Stars.

#fliptheswitch – to share changes and positive actions you are taking to reach your ideal life.

#mind-morph – include the Mind-Morph tag any time you'd like to!

You can also send an email to MyLifeTBDbyMe@mind-morph.com, where we celebrate your successes with you.

Don't underestimate your value as an individual and as a contributor to the greater good.

Your friend in change,

Chris Doyle

SUPPLEMENTS

Achievement Annihilators

Below is a list of common *achievement annihilators*, issues that will block your chances of success, fulfillment, achievement, and all things which encompass an abundant life. When you find yourself in Section B of the **ABCs of the Mind-Morph Mechanism** during any portion of your Mind-Morph journey, take a look and see if one of these annihilators is holding you back.

You will notice I've left plenty of space for you to write other annihilators as well. They can be different for all of us depending on where we are in the process and what we are trying to achieve.

If you insert your other annihilator(s), be sure to identify how each one is causing you to have a limited mindset. Then, find a way to change it to foster a growth mindset. Use Section C of the **ABCs of the Mind-Morph Mechanism** to categorize the annihilator into one of the three Resolution Paths. And, finally, you can annihilate the annihilator! Blow it up! Knock it out of your life and out of your path to achieving!

Common Achievement Annihilators

Annihilator	Limited Mindset	Growth Mindset	Resolution Path
Fear	I can't because I'm afraid of (insert fear).	I'm afraid that I'm not going to let it stop me.	Acknowledge the fear, then let it go and clear it out.
Perfection	It isn't complete because it's just not right yet.	It's perfect just the way it is, and I can always keep improving.	Reset, Reflect, Realign
Confusion	I have no idea what I'm doing or where to start.	I'm going to start with a great plan.	What's Your Why?
Excuses	No one around me wants me to succeed.	I'm happy with my goals and plans for myself.	Reset, Reflect, Realign
Momentum	I had to stop for a while and now I can't get going again.	I needed a little break, and now I'm ready to go!	Reset, Reflect, Realign
Distraction	I'm too busy with everything else in life.	I'm important and need time for me.	Reset, Reflect, Realign
Comparison	My work isn't as good as my competitor's.	My work gets better and better.	What's Your Why?
Comfortable	Why take a risk with no guarantee of success?	It's a little risky, and I'm going for it.	What's Your Why?
Stuck	I'm in a rut and can't get out.	This is going to be big, and I need to keep going.	What's Your Why?
Validation	I can't do it if my close friends don't think it will work.	I'm going to do it because I think I will succeed.	Acknowledge the fear, then let it go and clear it out.

Common Achievement Annihilators

Annihilator	Limited Mindset	Growth Mindset	Resolution Path
Uncertainty	I'm not going to try it because I don't know if it will work.	Win or lose; it's worth a shot!	Acknowledge the fear, then let it go and clear it out.
Knowledge	I don't know enough about it.	I'm going to learn everything I can.	Acknowledge the fear, then let it go and clear it out.
Planning	I don't think I have a good plan, so I better wait.	Everyone starts with that first step.	Acknowledge the fear, then let it go and clear it out.

Write in your personal Achievement Annihilators below.

Take Action Survey

If you find you are unsure where to start with taking action toward your life-change or if you feel stuck within your action items, take this little survey to give yourself some ideas for getting into positive motion.

Reminders

- Approach this activity as if you have no idea where to start or you are rebooting and starting from the beginning.
- Look back at your answers throughout each chapter and refine it if needed. You are already engaged in the process of taking action by capturing answers/thoughts/desires throughout this book.
- There is magic to the process of physically writing your action items rather than typing them on a computer. You can certainly put a final version on your computer if you desire, however go through your brainstorming, recording your thoughts and making your list by hand first.
- You are not asking specifically how this is going to occur. Be open to the suggestions and offerings in whatever way they may come.

Survey

Answer these questions as thoughtfully and completely as you can. Use extra paper if you need additional room. Complete the survey in a quiet space with little interruption. If you can complete the survey in one sitting, it will allow you to have continual, uninterrupted thought-flow allowing you to reach as deep as you can and to be completely thorough. Approach the survey as an *experience*, not a **task**; there is no right or wrong answer.

Throughout the survey, I will offer some context examples. For the examples, I will use the scenario of someone who is putting action around losing weight.

1) Describe why you believe your desire is achievable.
   Example: I believe I can lose the weight I want because it is not a physical, mental, or emotional impossibility for me. I have a support system and a plan that will help me achieve my desired weight.
   Your Belief: _____
   _____
   _____

2) What is your ask?
   a. Be specific. Don't just say that you are asking

to lose weight. Specifically, ask to lose 20 pounds.

b. The ask is exactly that – an ask. It is not a statement. Don't state, "I'd like to lose 20 pounds." Ask, "How can I lose 20 pounds? Will you help me lose 20 pounds?"

Example: (God, Universe, Higher Power), I know I can reach my desired weight with your help. Will you please provide the way, make it easy and give me the willpower to lose 20 pounds?

Your Ask: _____

_____

_____

3) What is your why?

a. Get honest and real here. If you think the reason you want to lose 20 pounds is so you can wear designer clothes, well sure, that is a reason. I might challenge that a bit. Think about why you want to wear designer clothes.

b. You might then say something like, "If I am wearing designer clothes, then women will pay more attention to me when I am out with my friends." Why do you want women to pay more attention to you?

c. "Because I want to be in a good, long-term relationship." Ah-ha! That revelation is your REAL why. Be sure you connect to the real reason you are asking. Connecting to the reason is important!

d. **NOTE: If you are struggling with your WHY, see the supplement titled <u>Finding My Why</u>.**

Example: I want to lose 20 pounds because I will feel better about myself and finding a lifelong partner.

Your Why: _____

_____

_____

4) Are your ask and your why in alignment?

Make sure your *ask* and your *why* is spiritually and universally aligned. For example, if you ask to lose weight, and the reason why is to buy new designer clothes, is there perfection and purpose between the ask and the why? Is it in alignment with your beliefs and your real reasons for asking?

Example: Losing weight to feel better about me and finding a life partner is in alignment with my core values. I value being fit and healthy as well as finding a companion who will appreciate me for who I am.

Your Alignment: _____

_____

_____

5) What does achieving this look like to you?

Be detailed. In my losing weight example, this might look like a certain number on the scale, certain clothing size and a certain percentage of body fat. It also looks like being with the love of your life, enjoying your day-to-day, having someone who will also share this journey with you.

Example: Reaching my desired weight is seeing a 20-pound drop on the scale and losing 2 belt sizes. It is also feeling GREAT about my health and sharing continued fitness with someone I love.

Your Result: _____

_____

_____

6) What does a person look like that has achieved what you are striving for?

>Think of someone you know or admire who has perhaps achieved the same thing you wish to achieve or experienced the same struggles you have to reach their achievement.

Example: Steve looks great after his weight loss experience. His clothes fit much better on him now. His whole mood and persona are much more positive about everything than they were before because he feels better about himself and has a lot more confidence. His confidence is allowing him to attend more group functions and social gatherings, and he is meeting more people with who he could have a serious relationship. Steve is a good model of what I want to become.

Your Role Model: _____

_____

_____

7) What do you think that person did/does to get that result?

Example: I feel like Steve is unquestionably committed to his weight loss. He talks about his new routine with those around him. He weighs and measures his food portions. He celebrates when he sees positive results. He has also started working out and running.

Your Role Model's Efforts: _____

_____

_____

8) Now, how can you incorporate those concepts for yourself?
    a. What do you need to know to be like that person?
    b. What resources do you need?
    c. What does your mindset (mind-change need to be)?
    d. Can you find a mentor and/or build a support network?

Example: To have the same kind of success Steve has had, I am going to get more serious about my weight loss, stop procrastinating, and become committed to reaching my desired weight by hiring a personal trainer.

_____
_____
_____

9) When do you want to receive it?

It is important to be specific about when you want to receive your desire. For example, don't just ask to lose 20 pounds. Specifically, ask and/or set the goal date.

Example: I will continue to believe, ask, and act to reach my desired weight by eating healthy and exercising between and now and the holidays.

Your Timeframe: _____

_____
_____

10) What are your inspired actions?

a. These actions are your list of activities that will help you reach your achievement.

b. Be sure to include something about positive attraction. Remember, positive attracts *positive*, not necessarily positive, attracts the ***result***.

Example: In order to reach my desired weight, I will A) Positively attract the will power, the commitment and everything I need to be successful, B) Get on a meal plan with a nutritionist, C) Join the health club and D) Ask Steve if he would help me on my weight loss journey.

Your Inspired Actions: _____

_____

_____

11) Of all the activities which ONE is the one that feels best to do now?

    Choose one now, then go back and choose another one each week.

Example: I am going to start by asking Steve if he will help me.

First Step: _____

_____

_____

12) Acknowledge your readiness to receive.
    a. Can you take action now?
    b. Are you in alignment with everything around

you, including positive people, feeling good about your job/career, and feeling positive because of the energies of the universe?

Example: I am ready to receive this gift of losing weight, feeling better about myself, and finding a life partner.

Your Acknowledgement: _____

_____

_____

13) Perform daily "check-ins."
   a. When will you perform your check-in?
   b. What is going well?
   c. What needs improvement?
   d. What is your why?

Example: I'm doing good today with my nutrition plan. I need to follow-through on my commitment to working out. I sincerely want this for myself because I believe it will help me get to a point where I will find my life partner.

Your Check-In: _____

_____

_____

Finding My Why

At times connecting with the real reason *why* you are doing something can be quite a challenge. Every parent has likely asked the question, "Why did you do that?" to a child. More often than not, whether you ask a toddler, a pre-teen, or a young adult, the reply is, "I don't know."

Considering the human brain doesn't fully develop until the age of 25, not knowing why we've done something might be completely understandable. At the age of about 5, my son came to me one day and said, "Dad, doing this hurts my face." He then contorted his face in an obviously painful way. It struck me as funny, and I nearly fell off the couch laughing. Then I asked, "Why are you doing that?" His response? "I don't know." He honestly did not have any idea why he was doing it.

As adults, we often think we need to have the answers for everything. Especially when it comes to our personal needs, feelings, and actions. Not knowing why we want something is troubling. I suspect, as I've discussed throughout the book, this is a learned, conditioned behavior that we can overcome. It is part and parcel of our rapid thinking process and desire to come to a solution quickly – regardless of how shallow that solution may be.

For example, if you see a colleague at work first thing in the morning, you might wish them a hearty "Good morning!" The pleasantry will continue with, "How are you today?" After this, you will likely receive a response similar to "I'm great." Conditioned. Quick. Resolved. Time to move on. However, if you were to take a few more minutes to determine if the response was sincere, you might find a more *real* reply. Now the conversation could sound similar to this:

YOU: "Good morning! How are you today?"
COLLEAGUE: "I'm great."
YOU: "Are you great, or are you just saying that?"
COLLEAGUE: "Well, now that you mention it, there is something that has been bothering me."

Can you see the difference I am pointing out by just asking one more simple question?

The 5 Whys

There is a set of strategies that help manufacturing businesses improve their processes known as Six Sigma. Six Sigma techniques are designed to reduce defect error rates greatly. Part of Six Sigma teaching is to determine the root cause of an issue using the **5 Whys**. Using the 5 Whys methodology, that is to say, asking *why* 5 times facilitates a more rapid discovery of root cause issues where actionable resolutions can are applied to stop the error from happening in the future.

Here's a simple example which applies to my teenage son:

PROBLEM: The school report card arrived with a 'D' in Spanish class.

1. Dad asks, "**Why** is there a 'D' in Spanish class?"
   Son responds, "I didn't do well on the mid-term."

2. Dad asks, "**Why** didn't you do well on the mid-term?"
   Son responds, "I don't have a lot of time to study."

3. Dad asks, "**Why** don't you have time to study?"
   Son responds, "By the time I get home from activities, I rest for a while, and then I'm too tired."

4. Dad asks, "**Why** are you so tired?"
   Son responds, "Because I get involved in playing video games, and I stay up too late."

I was able to get to the bottom (root cause) of this why exercise in 4 steps, instead of 5, though I could easily have asked another why question. Why does he choose to play video games instead of doing homework? However, I consider that question similar to asking, "What color is the red firetruck?" It's red. The answer is obvious, just as it is obvious that he'd much rather play video games than do homework.

By the time I got to the root cause – video games – an actionable resolution is made apparent. Stop playing video games to improve the grade in Spanish class.

That's the Six Sigma root cause methodology. How can we apply that to obtaining our Morph-Star and creating an ideal life? We can do that by changing the Six Sigma *problem* to your **Morph-Star** and changing the *root cause* to your most personal **why**.

A 5 Whys Mind-Morph Example

Here's that example again, except this time, let's assume my son has determined his Morph-Star is to get a better grade in Spanish, and he's trying to determine why he wants a better grade.

MORPH-STAR: To get a better grade in Spanish class.

1. Q: **Why** do I want a better grade in Spanish class?
   A: I need to pass the class.

2. Q: **Why** do I need to pass the class?
   A: I want to improve my grade point average.

3. Q: **Why** do I need a better GPA?
   A: To qualify for a good college.

4. Q: **Why** do I want to qualify for a good college instead of just an average college?
   A: I want to be able to get a better job when I graduate.

5. Q: **Why** do I want a better job?
   A: It will create more opportunities for me as I start my career.

Take notice of a few items in this example:

- Notice my son's first response. It is likely the off-the-cuff answer he gives to anyone that asks him why he needs to get a better grade. It is the quick, shallow, not-well-thought-out response. It also surrounds the "success" aspect, i.e., I want to succeed in Spanish.
- By the time he gets to the 5th why he has discovered the real reason he wants his Morph-Star and created an intimate connection to it.

"Success" or "Connection" as a Why?

In many instances, our initial why has more to do with our perception of success and less to do with our connection to the reason. This perception can come in the form of money, fame, recognition, etc. Beneath the surface, there is usually something within our consciousness, which, if thoughtfully exposed, will reflect our *real* why – our connection to the reason.

In his book *Start With Why*, Simon Sinek explains the pursuit of success, in and of itself, will ultimately be a fruitless effort. However, when the *why* is your motivation, success will naturally follow. He further explains it is our connection to our why that drives a passionate endeavor. The connection is also why we make purchasing decisions the way we do.

If you needed to buy a new mattress for your bed, you might talk to a salesperson who wants to sell you a mattress for $500. This salesperson will tell you all about the great construction, how the materials are the best in the industry, and that the mattress comes with a lifetime warranty. All impressive characteristics, and you still won't buy it because you think to yourself, "Is all of that worth 500 of my hard-earned dollars?"

Now let's say you walk into the mattress store directly across the street. When you walk into the store, the first mattress you see costs $1,000. Whoa! That is $500 more than the first one. However, the salesperson approaches and asks, "Why do you want to buy a mattress?" You proceed to tell her your mattress is old, when you wake up you have a backache, and you don't feel well-rested. As you are invited to lay on the mattress, she continues by telling you that this mattress has received the highest ratings for comfort, and of those surveyed, the mattress receives praise for alleviating pains and provides more restful sleep. The salesperson then asks, "How much are you willing to invest for a more satisfying sleep, no more aches, and your overall personal health and wellbeing?"

At this point, most people could not deny that they would invest any amount of money in experiencing better health and restfulness, and suddenly $1,000 for a mattress is not a large sum at all. It doesn't feel like a large sum because the salesperson connected your real why to the purchase of the mattress. You aren't just buying a mattress; you are investing in a better life. This philosophy applies directly to why you are seeking your Morph-Star. Find your true connection to why you desire what you do and pursue it for that reason. When you do, success, wealth, fame, etc. will certainly follow.

Find Your Why

Work through the series of questions below as you seek the true reason for your Morph-Star. Remember these important concepts:

- Dig well below the surface. Your first answer is often not your deepest answer.
- Seek to follow your passion.

- Remain simple and clear in your statements.
- Take time to answer each question thoughtfully.
- Follow each WHY step. Don't skip directly to the end.

➤ Describe your Morph-Star.

Example: I am looking for a better job.

_____

_____

_____

➤ Why do you want it? The answer should be your first, initial reason, and perhaps what you generally tell most people if they ask.

Example: I need to make more money.

_____

_____

_____

➤ Take your answer and turn it into a *why* question. Then, answer that question.

Example: Q: Why do I need to make more money?
          A: I'm behind on my bills, and my finances are getting worse.

Q: _____

_____

SUPPLEMENT/FINDING MY WHY 233

A: _____

_____

➢ Take your previous answer and turn it into a *why* question. Then, answer that question.
   Example: Q: Why am I behind on my bills?
   A: I have two car payments, rent, two cell phones, gas, groceries, clothing, etc.

Q: _____

_____

A: _____

_____

➢ Once more, take your previous answer and turn it into a *why* question.
Then, answer that question.
   Example: Q: Why do I have two car payments, rent, etc.?
   A: It is important to me that my family has what they need from day-to-day.

Q: _____

_____

A: _____

By your 5th why, you should be able to see your *connection* and your real **why**. In this example, the reason for wanting the Morph-

Star of finding a better job is not to make more money (the success), rather to give your family what they need (the connection).

Never give up on finding the real reason you want something. Why you want it is as important as all of the other fundamentals presented here for finding success with Mind-Morph.

The Mind-Morph Water Butterfly

What's the significance of the Water Butterfly on the front cover of the book? Well, I am glad you asked...

My astrological sign is Pisces – a water sign. The characteristics of Pisces describe me perfectly: compassionate, artistic, intuitive, musical, and more.

Pisces are typically known as water lovers. I love water – lakes, swimming pools, the ocean. I find comfort in the sound water makes lapping against a shore or in a rushing mountain stream.

While it seems like my mind is always moving about a hundred miles an hour, I could probably sit, look, listen, and daydream at the edge of a pond for an entire day.

Water is symbolic, especially in spiritual terms. Mind-Morph embodies the essence of the symbolism in full immersion baptism by water, for example. When you rise from the water after baptism, you are symbolically clean and spiritually changed – a change of heart, mind, and life.

The ripples dancing across the top of the lake after throwing a stone in it will impress the mind of the long-lasting and far-reaching effects of our actions in life. Whether those actions be good or not, there is no way for us to stop the momentum of the results they bring in all directions. A reminder for us to keep our actions, and our words, good.

Butterflies go through what is called complete metamorphosis. They start as something different – a caterpillar. The change a caterpillar goes through in the cocoon (also called a chrysalis) is amazing. It turns from a caterpillar, into kind of a gooey protein liquid, then into a butterfly.

Once it has reached the butterfly stage and is ready to fly, it is time to come out of the cocoon. ***And here's the important part:*** The butterfly must struggle out of the cocoon. I know that might sound weird, however it must endure the struggle to fully complete its growth (change) to have the ability to fly.

Talk about Mind-Morph symbolism! Does that sound at all like anything you've had to do in life or through your change while reading this book? Have you had to kick and fight through a challenge, turmoil and/or despair? If you have, then you are growing. If you have, then the struggle has been an essential part of your change. If you have, then you are now ready to fly!

Notes & References

Mind-Morph 101

3   *For Love of the Game.* Directed by Sam Raimi, Universal Studios, 17 Sep. 1999.

6   *Marvel Cinematic Universe.* Marvel Studios, LLC, Walt Disney Studios.

Chapter 1: 7 *Pretty Simple* Fundamentals to Change Your Life

9   "Quotes by Amelia Earhart." *Amelia Earhart,* The Family of Amelia Earhart, 2018, www.ameliaearhart.com/quotes/.

12   "Theodore Roosevelt Biography in Brief." *The Roosevelt Center at Dickson State University,* Dickson State University, https://www.theodorerooseveltcenter.org/Learn-About-TR/TR-Brief-Biography.

12   "Theodore Roosevelt, Quotes, Quotable Quote." *Goodreads,* Goodreads, Inc., 2019, https://www.goodreads.com/quotes/9997-believe-you-can-and-you-re-halfway-there.

15   Chivers, Tom. "This Is Why You Still Cringe At The Memory Of Something You Did In School." *Buzzfeed,* Buzzfeed, Inc., 14 Apr. 2015, https://www.buzzfeed.com/tomchivers/whats-really-happening-when-a-decades-old-memory-makes-you-c?utm_term=.aiZJbAm6o#.nvvBKrvZe.

24   "Stevie Wonder Quotes." *BrainyQuote,* BrainyQuote, 2001-2019, https://www.brainyquote.com/quotes/stevie_wonder_120629.

26   Maxwell, John C. *Intentional Living: Choosing a Life That Matters.* Narrated by John C. Maxwell, Hachette Audio, 2015. Audiobook.

27   "Gillian Anderson Quotes." *BrainyQuote,* BrainyQuote, 2001-2019, https://www.brainyquote.com/quotes/gillian_anderson_129691.

34   Hill, Napoleon. *Think and Grow Rich: The Landmark Bestseller Now Revised and Updated for the 21st Century,* revised and expanded by Dr. Arthur R. Pell, The Penguin Group (USA), Inc., 2018.

40   Hill, Napoleon. *Think and Grow Rich: The Landmark Bestseller Now Revised and Updated for the 21st Century*, revised and expanded by Dr. Arthur R. Pell, The Penguin Group (USA), Inc., 2018.

Chapter 2: Can You Believe It?

47   American Idol is a registered trademark of Fremantle Limited (formerly FremantleMedia).

48   Ornstein, Robert, and Sobel, David. *The Healing Brain: Breakthrough Discoveries About How the Brain Keeps Us Healthy*. Malor Books, 1999. Print.

49   "Department of Psychology." *Texas Liberal Arts,* The University of Texas at Austin College of Liberal Arts, 2019, https://liberalarts.utexas.edu/psychology/faculty/markman.

58   "Gandhi's Birthday: 15 Inspiring Quotes." *Biography*, A&E Television Networks, LLC, 2019, https://www.biography.com/news/gandhi-quotes.

Chapter 3: Buckets of Laws

63   "Isaac Newton's Quotes." *Isaac Newton*, www.isaacnewton.org, 2015, http://www.isaacnewton.org/quotes.jsp.

72   "John Assaraf." *Goodreads*, Goodreads, Inc., 2019, https://www.goodreads.com/author/show/382239.John_Assaraf.

74   "The Einstein Letter That Started It All; A Message to President Roosevelt 25 Years Ago Launched the Atom Bomb and the Atomic Age." *The New York Times*, The New York Times Company, 2019, https://www.nytimes.com/1964/08/02/archives/the-einstein-letter-that-started-it-all-a-message-to-president.html.

75   DiSalvo, David. "Your Brain Sees Even When You Don't." *Forbes,* Forbes Media, LLC, 2019, https://www.forbes.com/sites/daviddisalvo/2013/06/22/your-brain-sees-even-when-you-dont/#6a962c01116a.

80   Andres, Andy. *The Butterfly Effect: How Your Life Matters*. Simple Truths, 2011. Print.

Chapter 4: #FlipTheSwitch

91   Tracy, Brian. "Blog." *Brian Tracy International,* Brian Tracy International, 2001, https://www.briantracy.com/blog/.

98   Chopra, Deepak. "Articles." *The Chopra Center,* The Chopra Center at Omni La Costa Resort and Spa, 2019, https://chopra.com/articles/how-does-karma-affect-your-life.

Chapter 5: Ready, Set, GET

114   "The Science." *mindsetworks,* Mindset Works, Inc., 2017, https://www.mindsetworks.com/Science/Default.

118   Kounang, Nadia. "What is the science behind fear?" *Cable News Network,* Turner Broadcasting System, Inc. 2019, https://www.cnn.com/2015/10/29/health/science-of-fear/index.html.

121   Krakovsky, Marina. "Insights by Stanford Business." *Graduate School of Stanford Business,* Stanford Graduate School of Business, 2019, https://www.gsb.stanford.edu/insights/researchers-if-you-want-favor-ask-ask-again.

121   Cherry, Kendra. "Jean Piaget Biography (1896-1980)." *verywellmind,* About, Inc. (Dotdash), 2019, https://www.verywellmind.com/jean-piaget-biography-1896-1980-2795549.

Chapter 6: "Action" Isn't a Noun

135   Maxwell, John C. *Intentional Living: Choosing a Life That Matters.* Narrated by John C. Maxwell, Hachette Audio, 2015. Audiobook.

145   May, Cindy. "A Learning Secret: Don't Take Notes with a Laptop." *Scientific American,* Scientific American, A Division of Springer Nature America, Inc., 2019, https://www.scientificamerican.com/article/a-learning-secret-don-t-take-notes-with-a-laptop/.

Chapter 7: Reset, Reflect, Realign

157   "Nelson Mandela." *Goodreads,* Goodreads, Inc., 2019, https://www.goodreads.com/quotes/9041891-i-never-lose-i-either-win-or-learn.

158   "Thomas A. Edison." *Goodreads*, Goodreads, Inc. 2019, https://www.goodreads.com/author/quotes/3091287.Thomas_A_Edison.

166   Hoque, Faisal. "Taming The Last 10%: Lessons For Finishing Meaningful Work." *Fast Company,* Fast Company & Inc., Mansueto Ventures, LLC, 2019, https://www.fastcompany.com/3015925/taming-the-last-10-percent-lessons-for-finishing-meaningful-work.

167   "Reese Witherspoon Quotes." *BrainyQuotes,* BrainyQuote, 2001, https://www.brainyquote.com/authors/reese_witherspoon.

173   "Global Homelessness Statistics." *Homeless World Cup Foundation,* Homeless World Cup Foundation, 2019, https://homelessworldcup.org/homelessness-statistics/.

173   "Know Your World: Facts About Hunger and Poverty." *The Hunger Project,* The Hunger Project, 2019, https://www.thp.org/knowledge-center/know-your-world-facts-about-hunger-poverty/.

174   Rocky and Rocky Balboa are registered trademarks of Metro-Goldwyn-Mayer Studios, Inc.

179   "What is Tai Chi?" *Tai Chi for Health Institute,* Tai Chi for Health Institute, 2018, https://taichiforhealthinstitute.org/what-is-tai-chi/.

182   Little River Band. "Lady." *Sleeper Catcher,* Harvest Records, 1978.

Chapter 8: A Key to the Universe

189   "Paulo Coelho Quotes." *Goodreads*, Goodreads, Inc., 2019, https://www.goodreads.com/quotes/1005094-when-you-want-something-all-the-universe-conspires-in-helping-you.

191   Baer, Drake. "Malcolm Gladwell Explains What Everyone Gets Wrong About His Famous '10,000 Hour Rule'." *Business Insider,* Insider, Inc., 2018, https://www.businessinsider.com/malcolm-gladwell-explains-the-10000-hour-rule-2014-6.

192   "Barbara Fredrickson." *The Pursuit of Happiness,* Pursuit of Happiness, Inc., 2018, http://www.pursuit-of-happiness.org/history-of-happiness/barb-fredrickson/.

193   "Willie Nelson Quotes." *Goodreads*, Goodreads, Inc., 2019, https://www.goodreads.com/quotes/1017547-once-you-replace-negative-thoughts-with-positive-ones-you-ll-start.

198 Jacques, Renee. "16 Wildly Successful People Who Overcame Huge Obstacles To Get There." *HuffPost Life Wellness,* Verizon Media, 2019, https://www.huffpost.com/entry/successful-people-obstacles_n_3964459.

199 "Defeating The Odds: Famous People Who Overcame Rough Obstacles." *Hooch,* www.hooch.net, 2019, https://www.hooch.net/defeating-the-odds-famous-people-who-overcame-rough-obstacles/?view-all&chrome=1&D4cHN=1&D4cTCHN=1&D_4_6cALL=1&D_4_6_10cALL=1.

Finding My Why

225 Sather, Rita, RN and Shelat, Amit, MD. "Understanding the Teen Brain." *Health Encyclopedia,* University of Rochester Medical Center, 2019, https://www.urmc.rochester.edu/encyclopedia/content.aspx?ContentTypeID=1&ContentID=3051.

226 iSixSigma-Editorial. "Determine The Root Cause: 5 Whys." *iSixSigma,* iSixSigma, 2000-2019, https://www.isixsigma.com/tools-templates/cause-effect/determine-root-cause-5-whys/.

230 Sinek, Simon. *Start With Why.* Portfolio/Penguin, 2009. Print.

MORE TO COME

Look for these upcoming titles in the Mind-Morph series.

www.ingramcontent.com/pod-product-compliance
Lightning Source LLC
Chambersburg PA
CBHW032106090426
42743CB00007B/251